STUDENT'S BOOK
with Workbook Digital Pack

3

CEFR
B1+

D1930597

TH!NK
SECOND EDITION

Herbert Puchta,
Jeff Stranks &
Peter Lewis-Jones

CAMBRIDGE
UNIVERSITY PRESS

CONTENTS

WELCOME

A THAT'S ENTERTAINMENT!

let and *allow*

1 W.01 **Complete the conversation with the words. Then listen and check.**

allowed | cross | feel | get
guitar | let | look | ~~looking~~
makes | songs | sound | talent show

Sara Hey, Karl, what are you [0]*looking* at?
Karl My History book. Can't you see I'm busy?
Sara I'm just asking. Sorry.
Karl No, I'm sorry. I don't [1]______ great today.
Sara You don't [2]______ very happy. What's the matter?
Karl My dad [3]______ me so [4]______ .
Sara That doesn't [5]______ so good. Why?
Karl He says I'm not [6]______ to be in the band.
Sara What?! So he won't allow you to play in the [7]______ at the weekend?
Karl No. He says no music until after my exams.
Sara But that's four weeks from now!
Karl I know. He wants me to study and forget about writing [8]______ . He won't even [9]______ me practise the [10]______ .
Sara But you need some time to relax.
Karl I know. I [11]______ so angry when I think about it. It just isn't fair.

2 W.01 **Listen again. Answer the questions.**

1 Why is Karl angry?
2 How long is it until the exams finish?
3 What does Sara think about the situation?
4 Who do you agree with: Karl or his dad? Why?

3 SPEAKING **What do your parents allow you to do during exam time? What don't they let you do? Make lists. Then compare with a partner.**

Music

4 **Sort the words into two groups. Label the groups. Then think of four more items for each one.**

classical | drums | guitar | jazz
piano | pop | rap | violin

Verbs of perception

5 **Complete the sentences from the conversation with the correct forms of (*not*) *look*. Then match them with the rules.**

1 You ____________________ very happy.
2 Hey, Karl, what ____________________ at?

RULE: We use verbs of perception (*look, smell, feel, taste*) …
- in the present continuous to talk about actions. ☐
- in the present simple to talk about states. ☐

6 **Complete the mini-dialogues with the correct forms of the verbs.**

1 taste
A What are you doing?
B I ______ the soup … It ______ great.

2 smell
A My socks ______ really bad!
B Then why ______ you ______ them?

3 feel
A Why ______ you ______ that jumper?
B Because it's so soft. I like the way it ______ .

7 SPEAKING **Work in pairs. Karl tries to persuade his dad to let him play in the talent show. Write a conversation of eight lines. Then read it out.**

The big screen

8 SPEAKING **Work in pairs. For each type of film, think of an example that you have both seen.**

action | animated | comedy
drama | horror | romantic comedy
science fiction | thriller

9 **Read the article. What types of films does it mention?**

10 **Read the article again and answer the questions.**

1 When did Columbus start making films?
2 Who are his films especially popular with?
3 Where did he learn about filmmaking?
4 What does he do apart from direct films?
5 Who started a company with him?

11 SPEAKING **Work in pairs. Think of your favourite film director and discuss these questions.**

1 What films has this director made?
2 What do you like about his/her films?

Present perfect tenses

12 **Complete the sentences. Use the present perfect simple or continuous form of the verbs and choose the correct words.**

1 They have been playing (play) *for* / *since* 87 minutes and neither side has scored yet.
2 I *yet* / *still* haven't seen (not see) the final, so please don't tell me which singer won.
3 Have you seen (see) last night's show *still* / *yet*? Bradley Cooper and Lady Gaga were guests.
4 The children have been sitting (sit) in front of the TV watching *SpongeBob for* / *since* seven o'clock this morning.
5 It's the funniest programme on TV. I haven't missed (not miss) an episode *still* / *yet*.
6 The Prime Minister has been saying (say) the same thing *for* / *since* weeks now. No one believes her.

BEHIND THE CAMERA

CHRIS COLUMBUS

A 12-year-old who gets left behind when his family go on holiday, a teenage magician fighting to save his world and the troubled son of a Greek god living in modern-day America: these are just three of the characters brought to life on the big screen by director Chris Columbus. With films such as *Home Alone*, *Harry Potter and the Chamber of Secrets* and *Percy Jackson: Sea of Monsters*, Columbus has certainly shown that he knows how to get teenagers into the cinema.

Columbus, who studied film at New York University, has been making films for more than 30 years and has become one of the most successful film directors of all time. Since he directed his first film, *Adventures in Babysitting*, in 1987, Columbus has been involved in some of the biggest films as both a director and a producer.

But Columbus doesn't only make action films for the teenage market. He's also made a number of successful films for adults. Comedies such as *Mrs. Doubtfire*, dramas such as *The Help* and science fiction films such as *Bicentennial Man* have all helped make Columbus one of Hollywood's most popular filmmakers. And in 2014, he formed a production company with his daughter Eleanor.

TV programmes

13 SPEAKING **Work in pairs. Look at the sentences in the previous exercise. Match them with the types of TV programme.**

cartoon 4 | chat show 3 | sitcom 5
sports programme 1 | talent show 2 | the news 6

14 **Choose a type of TV programme from the list below. Write a sentence about it using the present perfect simple and/or continuous. Don't include the type of programme in your sentence!**

drama series | game show
reality show | soap (opera)

I've been watching it for weeks, but no one has won the million-dollar prize yet.

15 SPEAKING **Read out your sentence. Can the rest of the class guess the type of TV programme?**

B TIME TO ACT

Our endangered planet

1 SPEAKING **Work in pairs. Describe the photos. What problems do they show?**

A

B

C

2 W.02 **Listen to three conversations. Match them with the photos.**

3 W.02 **Listen again. In which conversation do you hear these words? Write the number.**

a rubbish ☐
b climate change ☐
c litter ☐
d pollution ☐
e fumes ☐
f smog ☐
g flooding ☐

Question tags

4 **Complete these sentences from the recording with the question tags.**

~~are they~~? | ~~aren't they?~~ | ~~does it?~~ | ~~did they~~? | is it? | isn't it? | ~~weren't they~~? | ~~doesn't it?~~

1 I guess they're just lazy, aren't they?
2 But it only takes a few people to spoil everything, doesn't it?
3 Yes, it's all those fumes from the factory, isn't it?
4 They didn't ask us if we wanted it here, did they?
5 Even if they do, it doesn't make our lives any better, does it?
6 Hundreds of homes were damaged, weren't they?
7 And the politicians aren't really doing anything to help, are they?
8 It isn't the sort of thing you'd expect to see here, is it?

5 **Complete the sentences with question tags.**

1 You haven't told Ron, __________ ?
2 You're going to do something about it, __________ ?
3 It sounds quite dangerous, __________ ?
4 It didn't work, __________ ?
5 It won't be easy, __________ ?
6 She wrote to her local politician, __________ ?

So do I / Neither do I

6 **Look at the questions and complete the answers with *so* or *neither*.**

1 A I don't really believe in all that.
B Neither do I.
2 A I think we should do something.
B So do I.

7 SPEAKING **Complete the sentences so that they are true for you and read them out. Agree (or disagree!) with your partner's sentences.**

1 I really like __________ .
2 I don't like __________ .
3 I believe __________ .
4 I don't believe __________ .

Accepting and refusing invitations

8 W.03 **Put the sentences in order to make a conversation. Then listen and check.**

[1] **Mandy** Marco and I want to do something to help the flood victims.
☐ **Mandy** Yes – 20 km! Want to join us?
☐ **Mandy** That's a shame. But you will sponsor us, won't you?
☐ **Mandy** We're going to do a sponsored walk next Sunday.
☐ **Jamal** Of course I will.
☐ **Jamal** Are you going to walk a long way?
☐ **Jamal** What are you going to do?
☐ **Jamal** I'd love to, but I can't. I'm busy.

9 SPEAKING **Work in pairs. Write a conversation using the underlined phrases from Exercise 8.**

You and your friend are tired of all the rubbish in the street and have decided to do something about it. What are you going to do? Invite another friend to join you.

Party time

10 **Work in pairs. Imagine you're organising a party. Make a list of important things to do.**

11 **Read the article. Does it mention the things on your list?**

HOW TO PLAN A PARTY

The first question to ask is, 'Why am I having a party?' (It's someone's birthday; it's the end of term; your team won a big championship; just to have fun with friends.)

A really good party has a theme. What's going to be the theme for yours? Beach party? 1970s disco? Something else? Then you have to find [1] somewhere to have your party. Wherever you decide to have it, it's always a good idea to [2] get permission from your parents first.

Now, it's time to [3] draw up the guest list. Are you going to invite [4] everyone you know, or just some of your friends? It's important to think hard about how many people you can afford to invite. Once your list is ready, you can [5] send out the invitations. A good time is about a fortnight before the party. Any sooner, and people might forget about it; any later, and some of the people on your list might already have other plans.

OK, so now you've got two weeks to get everything ready. Don't panic – it's plenty of time: just don't leave [6] everything until the last minute. If you want to [7] hire a DJ, start looking now. Remember that they might ask you to [8] pay a deposit, so make sure you've got money for that. Then you need to [9] organise the food and [10] decorate the room, although these things can be left until the day before.

Last but not least, keep cool, get some sleep, and in the afternoon before the party, just check it's all ready. Then – have fun!

12 **Read the article again and complete it with the missing words.**

decorate | draw up | everyone | everything | get | hire | organise | pay | send out | somewhere

Indefinite pronouns

13 W.04 **Complete the conversation with suitable indefinite pronouns (*everyone, somewhere, nothing*, etc.). Then listen and check.**

David Have you got [1] ______ ready for the party?

Joanna No, [2] ______ is ready. We haven't found [3] ______ to have it, for a start. We've looked [4] ______ .

David Have you invited [5] ______ yet?

Joanna Yes, we've invited 50 people and [6] ______ is coming!

David So you've got 50 people coming, but [7] ______ for them to come to?

Joanna That's right.

David Well, we've got to do [8] ______ . How about using my house?

Joanna What about your parents?

David They won't mind. They're going [9] ______ for the weekend. I'll make sure [10] ______ is clean and tidy when they get home.

14 **Read the next part of the story and continue the conversation. Write four more lines. Use at least one indefinite pronoun.**

It's the day after the party. David's mum and dad arrive home and open the door ...

Mum What's happened? Look at our house!

Dad David! DAVID!

David Oh, hi, Mum. Hi, Dad. You're home early. Did you have a good time?

Arranging a party

15 SPEAKING **Work in pairs to organise a party. Be creative! Think about:**

- what it's for
- the theme
- who to invite
- where it will be
- food and drink
- music

C IN MY OPINION, ...

Feeling under the weather

1 W.05 **Listen to the conversation. What's the matter with Angie?**

2 **Complete the conversation with the words.**

appointment | better
energy | get | operation
physically | should | took

Mum You don't look well, Angie. What's up?

Angie I'm just tired all the time, Mum. You know, I haven't got any [1]______ .

Mum Are you sleeping OK?

Angie Not great, no. I often wake up in the night.

Mum Well, you know, Angie, you [2]______ take more exercise. That would help.

Angie Really?

Mum Yes. I mean, if you [3]______ more exercise, you'd be more tired [4]______ and then you'd sleep better.

Angie You're joking, right? I run, I go swimming, I go for long walks. My problem isn't exercise.

Mum Yes, you're right, of course. Well, perhaps you'd [5]______ see a doctor. I can ring and make an [6]______ for you if you like.

Angie A doctor? I don't think so. I don't feel sick – just tired. I'm sure I'll [7]______ better soon.

Mum OK, well, we can talk about it later. I'm going out to see a friend of mine who had an [8]______ last week.

Angie OK, Mum. Hope your friend's all right. And don't worry about me. I'll be fine.

3 **Match the verbs (1–6) with the nouns and adjectives (a–f) to make phrases. Sometimes there's more than one possible combination.**

1 feel	a an appointment
2 get	b an operation
3 have	c exercise
4 make	d a doctor
5 see	e better
6 take	f sick

4 **Write down as many words related to health as you can think of. Then compare with a partner.**

sick
nurse
hospital
...

Giving advice

5 **Complete the sentences with *better*, *should* or *ought*.**

1 It's late – you'd ______ go.
2 If you aren't well, you ______ to see a doctor.
3 Jane's in hospital. We ______ go and visit her.
4 The doctor is very busy, so you ______ make an appointment. Don't just turn up.
5 Your knee hurts? Well, you'd ______ not play football today, then.
6 If you want to get better, you ______ to rest as much as possible.

6 **Match the problems (1–3) with the advice (a–c). Then write one more piece of advice for each problem. Use *had better*, *should* and *ought to*.**

1 My hand really hurts. ☐
2 I think I'm going to be late for school. ☐
3 I can't do this homework. ☐

a You'd better hurry.
b Perhaps you should phone a friend.
c You ought to see a doctor.

7 SPEAKING **Work in pairs. Write mini-dialogues including the problems and advice in Exercise 6. Add two or three lines to each. Then act them out.**

Better or worse?

8 Read the blog entry. Mark the sentences T (true) or F (false).

1 The writer likes awards ceremonies. ☐
2 *A Star is Born* won Best Film at the 2019 Oscars. ☐
3 The writer thinks the song in *A Star is Born* is the coolest he's ever heard. ☐
4 Dave thinks the writer is very intelligent. ☐

9 SPEAKING Work in pairs. Discuss these questions.

1 What other awards ceremonies do you know of?
2 Do you like awards ceremonies? Why or why not?
3 Do you think it's fair to compare different movies, actors, music, etc. and choose one as the best?

Comparisons

10 Complete the sentences with the correct form of the adjectives and adverbs. Add any other necessary words.

1 The weather tomorrow won't be ________ (cold) as today.
2 This is the ________ (good) pizza I've ever eaten.
3 Do you think this is ________ (difficult) than the other test?
4 This book's OK, but it isn't the ________ (interesting) one I've ever read.
5 She learns things ________ (easy) than I do.
6 I'm not very good at tennis, but I'm ________ (bad) as Janice!
7 Hurry up! Can't you walk ________ (quick) than that?
8 Do you speak ________ (loud) as your sister?

11 SPEAKING Work in pairs or small groups. Discuss these statements. Do you agree or disagree with them? Why?

1 The best things in life are free.
2 If something is more expensive, it's always better.
3 It's more important to work hard than to play hard.
4 Exercise isn't as important as good sleep.

12 Choose two things or people from one of these categories. Write a paragraph comparing them.

sports that you like | actors that you like
towns or cities that you know
school subjects | books that you have read

WHY ALL THESE awards?

I'm really tired of awards ceremonies and prizes. Why do we have to compare things? Everywhere you look, there's something going on about who or what is 'the best' or 'the most comfortable' or 'the biggest', and so on. And sometimes the prize winners aren't the best anyway!

Here's an example: the Oscars in 2019. I saw the film *A Star is Born* and it was the most wonderful film I'd ever seen. But did it win the Oscar for Best Film? No! They gave the award to *Green Book*! Can you believe it? It wasn't as good as *A Star is Born*.

OK, *A Star is Born* got lots of nominations – seven, I think – but I don't think that's enough. Lady Gaga was fantastic as Ally Maine. In my opinion, I think she's much better than Olivia Colman, who won Best Actress. But the good thing is that *A Star is Born* won Best Original Song for *Shallow* – I've never heard anything as cool. And was the acting good? It was great! No other film had acting as brilliant as that.

I said all these things to my friend Dave the day after the Oscars. I told him I thought the judges were the craziest people in the world. Dave asked me how many films I'd seen in 2018. I said, 'One – *A Star is Born*.' Dave says he doesn't know anyone as silly as me.

D HELP!
Reported speech

1 **Read the story and answer the questions.**

1 What had happened to the caller's computer screen?
2 What three things did Vicky ask the caller to do?
3 Why couldn't the caller switch on the lights?
4 What did Vicky finally say to the caller?
5 What happened to Vicky in the end?

We asked readers to tell us about a time when they tried to help someone. Here's one from Vicky Hastings.

I used to work in IT for a big company, but I was fired because I got angry with a manager. Here's what happened.

I answered the phone one day and said, 'Hi. Can I help you?' A voice said, 'Hi. I'm a manager in the Sales Department and I've got an IT problem. I need your help.' 'What's the problem?' I asked, and he told me his computer screen had suddenly gone black.

[1]_____ , I couldn't think why it had happened. I asked him to check that the screen was still connected. He said it was. [2]_____ I asked him if he'd pressed any buttons by mistake. He said, 'No, I was downloading a program when, suddenly, it went "pooff".'

[3]_____ a few seconds, I said, 'OK, please check that your computer is still plugged in at the wall. Sometimes it gets disconnected accidentally.' The manager asked me to wait a bit. Then he came back and said, 'I can't see behind my desk where the plug is. It's very dark.' So I told him to switch the light on. Do you know what he said? 'Oh, I can't do that, the electricity went off five minutes ago.'

I tried to keep quiet. But [4]_____ , I had to say something. I warned him never to waste my time again, ever. He complained to my boss and I was fired. How fair is that, do you think?

2 **Rewrite the sentences in reported speech.**

0 'I need your help.'
He said that *he needed my help.*

1 'What's the problem?'
I asked him ________________

2 'I can't see here because it's very dark.'
He said that ________________

3 'Please check that your computer is still plugged in.'
I asked him to ________________

4 'I can't put the light on because the electricity went off five minutes ago.'
He said that ________________

Sequencing words

3 **Match these words with spaces 1–4 in the story.**

a After ☐ c finally ☐
b Then ☐ d At first ☐

Asking for and offering help

4 **Put the words in order to make questions.**

1 I / you / Can / help / ?
2 help / something / you / me / Could / with / ?
3 me / you / Can / a / lend / hand / ?
4 you / Do / help / any / need / ?
5 you / minutes / got / a / Have / few / ?

5 **Look at the sentences in Exercise 4 again. Mark them A (asking for help) or O (offering help).**

6 SPEAKING **Work in pairs. Choose a situation and write a conversation in which A asks B for help. Use expressions from Exercise 4. Then act it out.**

- A has a problem with some homework.
- A isn't feeling well.
- A's computer isn't working.
- A wants to have a party, but doesn't know where to hold it.

IT problems

7 SPEAKING Work in pairs. What do the pictures show?

A ☐

B ☐

C ☐

8 W.06 Listen to three conversations. Match them with the pictures in Exercise 7.

9 W.06 Listen again. In which conversation do you hear these words? Write the number.

a attachment ☐
b coverage ☐
c downloaded ☐
d file ☐
e install ☐
f online ☐
g program ☐
h upload ☐

IT vocabulary

10 Choose the correct words.

1 *go / have* online
2 *post / file* a message
3 *install / key in* your password
4 *install / go* a program
5 *attach / activate* a file
6 *go / download* a file
7 *upload / key* a photo
8 *key / delete* a message
9 *open / install* an attachment
10 *post / buy* an app
11 *upload / activate* flight mode
12 *have / go* network coverage

11 Match the verbs with the nouns. Make as many combinations as you can.

a message | a photo | flight mode | a password
an attachment | a program | a file | an app

0 install *install a program / an app*
1 attach ___
2 download ___
3 upload ___
4 open ___
5 post ___
6 delete ___
7 activate ___
8 key in ___

Passive tenses

12 Complete the sentences from the conversations with the verb forms.

is being repaired | was taken | is installed

1 The photo ___ on a safari trip.
2 Just click on it and the program ___ automatically.
3 The network ___ out here.

13 Rewrite the sentences in the passive.

0 Someone posted a message.
A message was posted.
1 Someone is downloading a program.
___
2 Someone has installed a new program.
___
3 Someone has keyed in the password.
___
4 Someone is repairing the anti-virus software.
___
5 Someone deleted the message.
___

14 Describe one of these processes using the passive.

- downloading an app to your mobile phone
- uploading a photo to a social networking site
- installing a program on your computer

1 BIG DECISIONS

OBJECTIVES

FUNCTIONS: talking about the future; complaining

GRAMMAR: present tenses (review); future tenses (review)

VOCABULARY: making changes; life plans; phrases with *up*

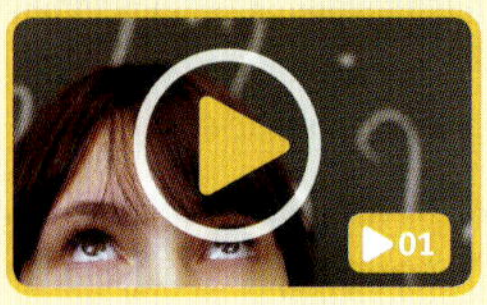

Get THINKING

Watch the video and think: are you good at making decisions?

A

B

C

D

E

READING

1 What are the people doing in the photos? Are these things you do or would like to do? Why?

2 Tick (✓) the things you would like to do when you finish school. Then add two more ideas of your own.

- 1 [✓] travel to other countries
- 2 [✓] go to university or college
- [ ] go into business
- [ ] get any job you can find
- [ ] do any job you can and spend time on your hobbies
- 4 [✓] find work that provides training on the job
- [ ] do volunteer work

3 + do a summer job

5 + get a year job before university

3 SPEAKING Work in pairs. Compare your ideas from Exercise 2. Give reasons for your choices.

4 Read John's blog post on the next page and the replies to it quickly. Which three photos show activities that these people do now?

Amy [ ] Mark [ ] Pauline [ ]

5 1.01 Read the article again and listen. Mark the sentences T (true) or F (false).

1 John is unsure what to do when he leaves school. T
2 John is worried about his exam results. F
3 Amy went to Thailand to learn the language. F
4 Amy has got plans for when she leaves Thailand. T
5 Mark's advice is to do a course. F
6 Pauline got a job before she finished her university course. F

What next?

John *posted 2 hours ago*

My time at school is almost up, and of course I'm thinking about the big question: what next? Perhaps I've left it a bit late to start thinking about it, but that's how I am. I think I'll do well in my exams, so maybe I'll go to university or college and get more qualifications – but I've been asking myself if it's better to just find a job and start a career that way. On the other hand, if I do go on to study further, should I do it right away or perhaps take a year off – a 'gap year'? Helpful comments and ideas, please! Thanks.

Like Share Reply

Amy *posted 5 minutes ago*

Hi, John. I'm doing a gap year right now. I saved up some money and went to Thailand, but after two months of 'holiday' I got bored and the money was running out. Then I learned about a volunteer medical organisation working in poor parts of the country and they let me join as a driver. Now I'm working, struggling with the Thai language (I spend up to an hour a day practising with friends) and learning lots about myself. I've made a resolution, too – when I go home, I'm going to study medicine, to be a doctor or a nurse. So my advice? Do a gap year, but don't just travel around – do some volunteer work somewhere. For me, it's been life-changing.

Like Share Reply

Mark *posted 28 minutes ago*

Hey! I left school three months ago and I didn't want to go to university or travel. So I'm doing a course. I'm studying to become a yoga teacher. I took up yoga a couple of years ago and I've loved it ever since. I was quite lazy at school, but I've changed my ways and now I study really hard. The course starts every day at 7.00, so I've had to get into the habit of waking up early. But that's fine – I love what I'm doing. That's the important thing – do what you love, if you can.

Like Share Reply

Pauline *posted 1 hour ago*

Hi there! Here's my advice. Do what feels right for you now, but keep an open mind and be prepared to change. Some of my friends went travelling after school, but I didn't have the courage; I just went to university. It was OK and I was having a good time. Then one day an old friend from school phoned me and said he was going to start an online company and asked me to join him. So, I gave up the university course and went to work with him. It was the best thing I've ever done. I wasn't intending to leave university, but I took the chance to try something different, and I don't regret it.

Like Share Reply

Train to TH!NK

Reading between the lines

Sometimes a writer doesn't tell us everything directly: we need to draw conclusions from the information the writer gives. We call this 'reading between the lines'.

6 Answer the questions and give reasons for your answers.

0 Is John worried about his abilities as a student?
No, he says he'll do well in his exams and he's thinking about university.
1 Has Amy been enjoying her work with a medical organisation?
2 Is Mark different now to when he was at school?
3 Did Pauline want to travel after leaving school?

SPEAKING

7 Work in pairs. Discuss these questions.

1 What resolutions are you going to make for this school year?
2 What do you think is the secret of changing your life for the better?

5 *Plan carefully.*
3 *Do work first, play later.*
6 *Listen to your parents.*

1 having a positive mindset
2 having a goal
4 being kind to receive kindness

GRAMMAR
Present tenses (review)

1 Match sentences (1–4) with the tenses (a–d) and then complete the rule with the names of the tenses.

1 I'm thinking about the big question: what next? c
2 I've been asking myself if it's perhaps better to just find a job. a
3 I spend up to an hour a day practising with friends. b
4 I've made a resolution. d

a present perfect continuous
b present simple
c present continuous
d present perfect

RULE:
We use the [5] __b__ to talk about something that happens regularly.
We use the [6] __c__ to talk about what's happening at or around the time of speaking.
We use the [7] __d__ to talk about past actions without saying when they happened.
We use the [8] __a__ to talk about actions that started in the past and are still happening.

Look
We can use the present continuous with *always* to complain about behaviour that we don't like and find annoying.
My dad's always telling me what to do.

2 Complete the text with the correct present tense forms of the verbs. Sometimes more than one tense is possible.

It's 2 am and I [1] __am lying__ (lie) in bed. I [2] __'m trying__ (try) to get to sleep, but I can't. I [3] __'m having__ (have) trouble sleeping for about a month now. I [4] __am trying__ (try) different things to help me sleep, but nothing [5] __is working__ (work). My mind [6] __doesn't want__ (not want) to stop. A lot [7] __is happening__ (happen) in my life right now. It's exam time, so I [8] __studying__ (study) a lot. There's also the question of next year. I [9] __'m thinking__ (think) about it for ages. Mum and Dad [10] __want__ (want) me to go to university, but I'm just not sure what to do.

3 SPEAKING Work in pairs. Think about a problem you've been having and tell your partner.

I've been fighting a lot with my little brother recently. I've tried to ignore him, but it's impossible.

→ workbook page 10

VOCABULARY
Making changes

4 Match the phrases with the definitions.

0 make a resolution f
1 give something up a
2 do well h
3 struggle with something d
4 take something up e
5 take the chance (*to do something*) c
6 get into the habit (*of doing something*) b
7 change your ways g

a stop doing something
b start doing something regularly
c use an opportunity
d find something difficult
e start a new hobby or interest
f decide to make a positive change
g do things differently (usually for the better)
h be successful

5 Complete the email with the missing verbs.

Sam
Sam@thinkmail.com

New Year's resolutions?

Last year I [1] __made__ loads of resolutions and decided to [2] __change__ my ways. I tried to [3] __get into__ the habit of getting up early. For two months I got up at 8 am, and I even [4] __took up__ running before going to school. But I started falling asleep in the afternoon, so I soon [5] __gave up__ that idea! Then I stopped eating meat. I was [6] __doing__ well until Mum made roast beef. I just had to eat it. I also [7] __took__ the chance to start learning the piano when my school offered extra classes. But I [8] __struggled__ with finding time to practise, so I stopped. This year I've only made one resolution: not to make any resolutions!

6 SPEAKING Work in pairs. Discuss these questions.

1 What subjects are you doing well in at school?
2 What subjects do you struggle with?
3 What was the last thing you gave up doing? Why?

→ workbook page 12

LISTENING

7 SPEAKING **Work in pairs. Discuss these questions.**

1 What do you know about these people?
2 Can you match the information with each person?

A Van Gogh was a famous painter.
B Carey Mulligan is a film actress.
C Walt Disney started a film studio.

8 1.02 **Listen and check.**

9 1.02 **Read the questions carefully. Listen again and make notes.**

1 What is Alan worried about?
2 Why does Becky tell Alan about Carey Mulligan?
3 Why was Walt Disney unsuccessful at first?
4 What does Alan not like about the example of Van Gogh?
5 How does Alan compare himself to Van Gogh?

10 SPEAKING **Work in pairs. Compare your answers to Exercise 9.**

Grammar rap!

GRAMMAR
Future tenses (review)

11 Look at the sentences from the listening. Complete them with the correct future forms of the verbs. Then complete the rule with the present continuous, *going to* or *will*.

1 We are having (have) a party at our place.
2 Are you going to apply (apply) to other drama schools?
3 I'm sure one of them will say (say) yes.

RULE:
- To talk about future arrangements, we often use the [4] present continuous.
- To make predictions, we often use [5] will.
- To talk about intentions, we often use [6] going to

12 Choose the best tense.

1 *We'll go* / *We're going to* the beach this Friday. Do you want to come?
2 I don't think *I'll finish* / *I'm finishing* this homework.
3 *I won't go* / *I'm not going* to university this year. I want to take a year off.
4 I've got an appointment with the dentist tomorrow. *I'm seeing* / *I'll see* her at 10 am.
5 Daisy's learning to fly. *She'll be* / *She's going to* be a pilot.
6 I'm not *eating* / *going to* eat chocolate. That's my resolution for next year.
7 Argentina *will win* / *are winning* the next World Cup. That's what I think.
8 *We're flying* / *We'll fly* on Friday. I'm so excited.

13 Write down:

1 two arrangements you've got for this week.
2 two intentions you've got for this year.
3 two predictions for your life.

→ workbook page 11

READING

1 SPEAKING **Tick (✓) the statements you agree with. Add one more thing you think is important. Then discuss in pairs.**

A good life means …

- ☐ getting rich.
- ☐ having friends who care about you.
- ☐ settling down and having a family.
- ☐ liking what you've got and not thinking about what you haven't got.
- ☐ doing work that's important for you.

2 1.03 **Listen and read the text. Put the phrases (a–f) into the correct spaces. Listen and check.**

a that's the point
b play live
c ~~really scares me~~
d a good experience
e is allowed
f raise money

3 SPEAKING **Work in pairs. Discuss these questions.**

1 Which of the things on this list would be on yours, too?
2 What other things would be on your 'before I settle down' list?

BEFORE I SETTLE DOWN – A LIST

A British billionaire once said: 'You only live once, but if you do it right, once is enough.' I love that quote, but what does 'doing it right' mean?

I suppose my grandparents did it right. They both left school, went to university (where they met) and got degrees. They started careers (he was an accountant, she was a doctor), then they got married and started a family. They got promoted at different times and then they both retired at 60. And off they went to travel the world. They've been happy, I think. However, it's just not really what I want – not yet, anyway. Before I settle down, when I'm 30 or so, I want to do all kinds of things. Here are some of them.

1 Do something that (0) ___c___ . I'm terrified of heights, so sky-diving would be perfect!

2 Sleep on a beach under the stars. Where? Somewhere warm, of course, where sleeping on the beach (1) ______ .

3 Take a really long train ride. The destination doesn't matter, it's the journey that's important. Train travel is brilliant – you can see the places you're passing through, you can meet and chat with other travellers, you can leave your seat and walk around. I love it!

4 Go somewhere where they don't speak English and I don't speak the language (Nepal?). It'll be hard, of course, but (2) ______ !

5 Run a marathon. I'm not a good runner and perhaps I'm not up to a marathon, but I'd really like to try. And perhaps I can (3) ______ for my favourite charity (cancer research).

6 Learn how to cook at least ten things that I love to eat. Right now I can only cook two!

7 Have dinner with a friend in one of the world's best restaurants.

8 See lots – lots! – of my favourite bands (4) ______ .

9 Do some kind of volunteer work for a while. In other words, work in order to help other people, not myself (though it'll be (5) ______ for me, too).

10 Make a list of other interesting things to do before I'm 40!

OK, that's my list. It's up to me to try to do these things. What would be on your list?

VOCABULARY
Life plans

4 Match the phrases with the pictures. Write 1–8 in the boxes.

1 retire
2 travel the world
3 start a career
4 get a degree
5 start a family
6 settle down
7 get promoted
8 leave school

5 Complete the text with phrases from Exercise 4. Use the correct forms of the verbs.

My uncle has always done things differently. He 1 ________________ when he was 18 because he wanted to see other places. He spent the next twenty years 2 ________________ , working in restaurants and hotels in many different countries. When he was in his early forties, he decided to return to the UK. He went to university and 3 ________________ . He did really well, and when he finished, he 4 ________________ as a translator. Because he was good at his job, he 5 ________________ quite quickly and he soon became Head Translator. When he was 48, he met the love of his life and they decided to 6 ________________ and 7 ________________ . Now he's 55, with three young children. He says he wants 8 ________________ soon. He wants to stop working and take the whole family around the world with him. I wouldn't be surprised if he does.

→ workbook page 12

WordWise: Phrases with *up*

6 Match the phrases in bold with the definitions.

1 **What's up**, Alan?
2 I spend **up to** an hour a day practising with friends.
3 What are you **up to** tomorrow night?
4 My time at school is almost **up**.
5 It's **up to me** now to try to do some of the things.
6 Perhaps I'm not **up to** a marathon.

a finished 4
b doing 3
c what's the matter? 1
d capable of 6
e as long as / to a maximum of 2
f my responsibility 5

7 Use words and phrases from Exercise 6 to complete the sentences.

1 What have you been up to recently?
2 The time is almost up . Two more minutes!
3 Oh, no! You look really unhappy. What's up ?
4 It isn't my decision. It's up to you to decide.
5 He's 75 now, so he isn't up to long walks.
6 This car can carry up to six people.

→ workbook page 12

PRONUNCIATION
Linking words with *up* Go to page 120.

WRITING
An email about resolutions

8 Write an email to an English-speaking friend in another country. Describe your resolutions for the coming school year. Write about:

- bad habits you're changing
- new classes you're taking
- activities you plan to take up
- why you're doing all of this

DEVELOPING SPEAKING

1 1.06 **Look at the photo. How is the girl feeling? Listen and read to check.**

Martin: Hi, Sandra. I haven't seen you for ages. Where have you been hiding?
Sandra: Hi, Martin. Hiding? Nowhere. I've just changed some of my routines. I was feeling so stressed a few months ago that I thought, 'Sandra, you've got to make some changes.' So I did!
Martin: What kind of changes? Exercise? Sleep?
Sandra: Well, where shall I start? I'm eating better. And now you mention it, I'm trying to get seven hours sleep a night, minimum. But the big thing is my attitude.
Martin: And how has that changed?
Sandra: Well, I read an article about stress and it said something like 'Look at the big picture. How important is this problem? Is it going to matter in three months' time?' And I thought, that's right – the problem is, I worry about little things too much. So I'm trying to worry less.
Martin: But can you do that? If I'm honest, I'm a terrible worrier, too. But I can't stop.
Sandra: Don't be silly. Anyone can stop worrying – not overnight, but you can do it little by little.
Martin: Now I'm getting stressed about being someone who can't stop worrying.
Sandra: Let's go and have ice cream and talk more.
Martin: Thanks, Sandra. You're a star.
Sandra: Here we go, then! Ice cream coming up! And don't worry, I'll pay!

2 1.06 **Read and listen again to the dialogue. Answer the questions.**

1 What areas of her life does Sandra say she's changed?
2 How much sleep is she trying to get?
3 What advice did she get from the article?
4 What is Martin getting stressed about?

3 SPEAKING **Discuss the questions in pairs. What do you think?**

1 Do things like diet and sleep help with stress?
2 Does the article give good advice? Why or why not?
3 Is it possible to slowly reduce how much you worry?

Phrases for fluency

4 **Find the underlined expressions in the dialogue. How do you say them in your language? Use the expressions to complete the conversations.**

1 A You look tired. Has it been a busy day?
B Busy? ______________________ ? First, I had a Maths test. Then I had Drama club at lunchtime. Then it was a five-kilometre run in PE …
A Well, you just sit down and I'll get you something to eat.
B Thanks, Mum. ______________________ .

2 A ______________________ , Annie? I haven't seen you for days.
B I haven't been anywhere. You're the one who disappeared.
A ______________________ , I have been quite busy.

3 A It's ten o'clock. Time for the test.
B ______________________ ! I'm really not ready for this.
A Me neither. I've got a feeling I'm not going to pass.
B ______________________ . You always pass.

FUNCTIONS
Expressing dissatisfaction

KEY LANGUAGE
I'm not happy with (my attitude).
The thing / problem is, (I worry too much).
If I'm honest, (I'm a terrible worrier, too).
My parents are always (telling me to work harder).

5 **Match the parts of the sentences.**

1 I'm not happy with ☐
2 He's always ☐
3 If I'm honest, ☐
4 The problem is, ☐

a he just laughs when I complain about it.
b I don't like his attitude.
c borrowing my things without asking me.
d the things my brother does.

ROLE PLAY **Work in pairs. Student A: go to page 127. Student B: go to page 128.**

LIFE COMPETENCIES

Stress can cause health problems, emotional problems and relationship problems. Finding ways to reduce or manage stress helps you feel healthier and happier, and be a better friend.

1 ▶ 03 **Watch the vlog. Why is Leo feeling stressed?**

2 ▶ 03 **Watch the vlog again and make notes about:**

a three symptoms of stress.

b three things you can do to deal with stress.

3 **Compare your notes with a partner.**

4 **Read this online article about stress. When can stress be useful?**

ALL ABOUT STRESS

We tend to think of stress as negative, but in fact it's something normal. Stress is our body's natural way of reacting to a difficult situation. Stress improves our ability to perform under pressure and to avoid danger. Cavemen hunting dangerous animals for food felt stress, and famous singers perform better on stage because of stress. However, stress becomes a problem when it reaches high levels and continues for a long period of time.

People seem to feel more stress these days. Money is one source of stress. Not having any money at all is very stressful, but for most of us, the problem is that we always want something better or newer. And we worry unnecessarily about things we can't afford.

Things like mobile phones can be a problem, too. We spend our lives moving from screen to screen, responding to a huge number of messages and images instead of really relaxing. Exercise is great for reducing stress, but technology in the form of smartphones and computers also means that we do much less exercise now than people did in the past.

The level of stress in our daily lives means that when we have to face really challenging situations, like doing exams or performing in public, our bodies are often less able to cope with them in a positive way.

5 SPEAKING **Work in pairs. Answer the questions.**

1 When does stress have a negative effect on us?
2 Why does the writer think people are more stressed these days?
3 Do you agree that the things mentioned in the article cause stress?
4 Can you think of any other reasons why people feel stressed?

Me and my world

6 **Make notes under the headings to show how your *family*, your *friends* and *school* might cause stress.**

FAMILY

____

____

____

____

FRIENDS

____

____

____

____

SCHOOL

____

____

____

____

7 SPEAKING **Think of a time when you were stressed. Talk to your partner about:**

- how you felt.
- what you did.
- what you would do differently in the future.

TIPS FOR MANAGING STRESS

- **Tell people how you are feeling. Being strong means sharing, not hiding feelings.**
- **Be patient – try not to worry about things you can't control.**
- **Get enough sleep and exercise, and eat healthily.**

2 A HARD LIFE

Get THINKING

Watch the video and think: would you like a demanding job when you leave school?

OBJECTIVES

FUNCTIONS: talking about the past

GRAMMAR: narrative tenses (review); *would* and *used to*

VOCABULARY: descriptive verbs; time periods

READING

1 **Look at the pictures and answer the questions.**

1 What do the pictures illustrate?
2 Where were the people from?
3 What happened to them?

2 **Read the article quickly. What is the big difference between James Ramsay and Mary Prince?**

3 2.01 **Read and listen to the article. Write R (Ramsay) or P (Prince) after each statement.**

1 Showed no discrimination R
2 Tried to escape their life P
3 Was separated from their parents when only a child P
4 Came from a family of slaves P
5 Was not popular with the local slave owners R
6 An event on a ship changed their life R
7 Their life became the subject of a book P
8 Helped slaves with their medical problems R

THEY MADE A DIFFERENCE

THE SLAVE TRADE

From the 16th to the 19th century, millions of people in Africa were taken from their homes and forced into lives of slavery. By the late 18th century many people had realised this was wrong and wanted to stop it. These people became known as 'abolitionists' and together they helped demolish one of the cruellest systems in the history of our world. Here are two of the men and women who made a huge difference.

One day in November 1759, the British ship *Arundel* was sailing the West Indies when a slave ship approached it, begging for help. Many of the slaves on the ship had died of disease and the others were living in horrible conditions. One person from the *Arundel* went to help – a young doctor called James Ramsay. He was horrified by what he saw and he never forgot this experience. Soon after this, he went to work on the island of St Kitts in the Caribbean. There he enraged local businessmen as he helped the slaves who worked for them and treated them for injuries and disease. He also worked as a church minister and he insisted on opening his church up to slaves as well as the white people. When Ramsay returned to England, he wrote books about his experiences. The vivid details he included shocked many people. He was also a huge influence on William Wilberforce, the leader of the anti-slavery movement in the UK and a politician who worked tirelessly to smash the laws and eventually succeeded in doing just that.

Mary Prince was born in Bermuda in 1788. As her mother and father were slaves she was a slave, too. She was sold a total of four times in her life. The first time with the rest of her family, but when she was 12, she was separated from them and went to work as a maid. She had been working at this job for a few months when she ran away to be with her mother, but she was soon captured and sent back. The third time she was sold to work in the salt ponds. The work was long and hard and the sun caused blisters on her body. She was also treated cruelly by her owners, who often struck her for the smallest of things. When she was 40, new owners took her to England. Slavery was illegal in the UK, so she was able to go and work with the abolitionists. In 1831, the Anti-Slavery Society published a book about her life story called *The History of Mary Prince*. Lots of people read the book and it helped many change their minds about slavery.

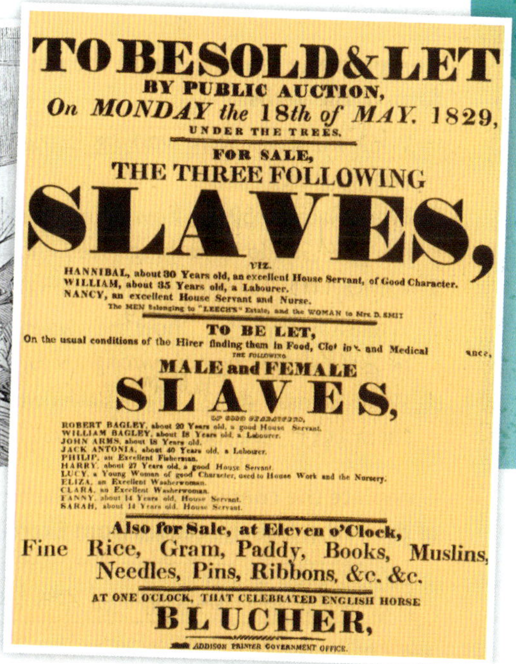

Train to TH!NK

Following an idea through a paragraph

It can be difficult to follow what a writer is trying to say in a longer paragraph. We need to read carefully to understand fully what the writer is saying.

4 Answer the questions.

In paragraph 2 it says: 'he wrote books about his experiences.'

1 Look back at the paragraph. What were his experiences? Make a list of them.

Near the end of paragraph 3 it says: 'the Anti-Slavery Society published a book about her life story.'

2 Look back at the paragraph. What things might the book include?

SPEAKING

5 Work in pairs. Discuss these questions.

1 Who would you suggest for the 'They Made a Difference' series?

2 Why would you include this person?

GRAMMAR
Narrative tenses (review)

1 Match the sentences from the article on page 21 with the tenses. Then complete the rule.

1 The British ship *Arundel* **was sailing** the West Indies when a slave ship approached.
2 Many of the slaves on the ship **had died of disease**.
3 She **had been working** at this job for a few months when she **ran away**.
4 In 1831, the Anti-Slavery Society **published** a book about her life.

a past perfect simple 2
b past simple 4
c past continuous 1
d past perfect continuous 3

RULE:
We use …
[5] b to talk about finished actions in the past.
[6] c to set the scene or to talk about longer actions in the past interrupted by shorter actions.
[7] a to talk about actions before a certain time in the past.
[8] d to talk about actions that continued for some time before a certain time in the past.

2 Complete the sentences with the past simple or past continuous form of the verbs.

0 While the slaves ***were working*** in the fields, a fire ***started***. (work / start)
1 When Ramsay saw how serious the situation was, he knew he had to do something. (see / know / have)
2 Ramsay was trying to help a slave when the man died. (try / die)
3 While Ramsay was watching how the owners treated the slaves, he started thinking how wrong it was. (watch / start)
4 While Ramsay was talking to the slave owners, many of them left the room. (talk / leave)

3 Complete the conversation with the correct form of the verbs. Use the tenses from Exercise 1.

~~burn~~ | ~~do~~ | ~~go~~ | ~~open~~ | ~~run~~ | ~~see~~ | ~~sit~~ | ~~walk~~

Ian I had a real scare yesterday. As I [1] was walking up to our house, I [2] saw smoke coming from the window.
Oli [3] Was something burning?
Ian Fortunately not. I [4] ran into the house, [5] opened the kitchen door and there was my brother. He [6] was sitting on the floor in shock. He [7] had been doing science experiments! One of them [8] had gone wrong and exploded.

→ workbook page 18

VOCABULARY
Descriptive verbs

4 Certain verbs make narratives sound more dramatic. Find these words in a dictionary and write down:

1 what they mean.
2 their past simple and past participle forms.

~~beg~~ | ~~demolish~~ | ~~enrage~~ | ~~force~~ | ~~shock~~ | ~~smash~~ | ~~strike~~

5 Replace the underlined words with words from Exercise 4. Change the form if necessary.

0 He was made to eat his vegetables by his mum. ***forced***
1 The sad news surprised the people. shocked
2 He asked urgently for help, but people just carried on walking. begged
3 It made me very angry when I heard what they had done. enraged
4 They knocked down the houses to make space for new shops. demolished
5 The car lost control and hit another vehicle. struck
6 He dropped the mirror and it broke into lots of pieces. smashed

→ workbook page 20

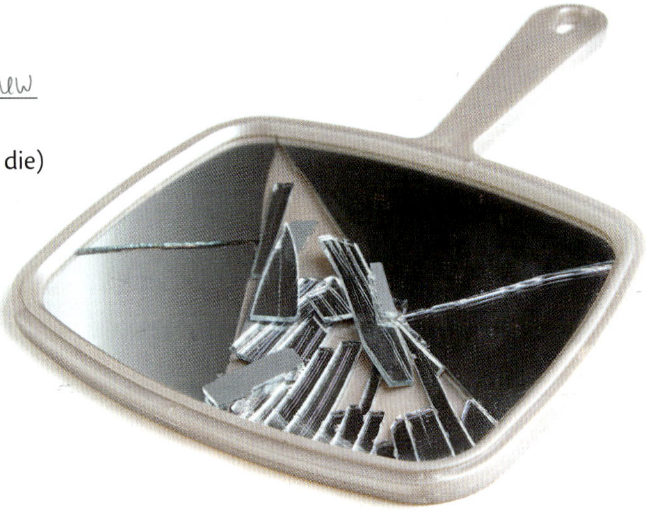

PRONUNCIATION
Initial consonant clusters with /s/
Go to page 120.

LISTENING

6 Look at the picture. Why is this bird special?

A It is the rarest bird in the world.
B It was once the most common bird in the world.
C It has a very unusual song.

7 2.04 Listen to the interview with Chris Oddie. Check your answer to Exercise 6 and answer these questions.

1 Who or what was Martha?
2 When was the last passenger pigeon seen in the wild?

8 2.04 Listen again. Choose A, B or C for each question.

1 What do we learn about passenger pigeons in Sarah's introduction?
   A They flew in enormous groups at night.
   B They lived up to the age of 50.
   C Their numbers dropped dramatically in the 19th century.
2 Which of these did not help lead to the extinction of the passenger pigeon?
   A a shortage of food
   B a big increase in hunting
   C better communication systems
3 Why did the US government law fail to help the passenger pigeon?
   A because people didn't respect the law
   B because no one cared about passenger pigeons
   C because they introduced the law too late
4 What does Chris hope we have learned from the extinction of the passenger pigeon?
   A All animals are equal.
   B Humans need to make sure animals are protected.
   C We need better programmes in zoos to help species in danger.

THINK values

Animal rights

9 Read the scenarios. Match them with statements 1–6. There are two statements for each scenario.

Scenario A: ☐ / ☐
Work on a huge multi-million-pound shopping centre has been stopped because nests of an extremely rare frog have been found in the area. It is one of only five places where this frog breeds. The property developers are putting pressure on the local government, saying it will be a disaster for the economy if they aren't allowed to finish the job.

Scenario B: ☐ / ☐
An elderly lady lives on her own. She has family, but they all live far away. A relative has suggested buying her a parrot for her 80th birthday. Other family members are against the idea of keeping an animal in a cage.

Scenario C: ☐ / ☐
There is a hotel that's very popular with tourists because it's close to a beautiful forest. The forest is home to a species of large spider. Although it's harmless, people working in the hotel have been given strict orders to kill any spiders that get into the guest rooms.

1 A bird in a cage can be a great companion for a person who lives alone, so it's the right present.
2 Creating places where people can relax is more important than worrying about a few animals.
3 We can't afford to lose any species of animal.
4 Places where endangered animals have their natural habitat belong to the animals, and not to people.
5 Spiders are ugly and disgusting, and many people are scared of them. Of course they should be killed.
6 Birds need to fly, and they need space to be able to do that. Cages should be forbidden.

10 SPEAKING Which of the statements 1–6 do you agree and disagree with? Why? Make notes of your answers. Then compare your ideas in pairs or small groups.

READING

1 SPEAKING Work in pairs. Look at the pictures. What are the problems with baths like these?

2 2.05 Read and listen to the article. Then check your answers.

A short history of bathing in the UK

These days most people in the UK have access to hot water by simply turning on a tap. People know how important it is to keep clean and take baths and showers daily. But of course, it wasn't always so easy.

In medieval times most people knew that washing your body with water was a good thing to do and there were instruction books that explained the importance of keeping your body clean. Some, though, offered rather strange advice, such as to avoid taking a bath in the summer or not to take long baths because they would make you fat.

In the palaces and houses of the rich, people enjoyed bathing in a wooden bathtub that servants filled with hot water. They would often add perfumes and flower petals to make the water smell nice. Having your own private bath was a sign of importance and King John, for example, used to take his bathtub with him whenever he travelled.

Most people had no bath of their own, but they might visit one of the many public baths that started to appear in most cities by then. These were often beside bakeries, and the heat from baking the bread was used to warm up the water.

People with no access to public baths would wash using only cold water and a cloth. When the weather was warm enough, they would jump in the nearest river for a wash.

By the early 1800s there were serious concerns about the dreadful conditions in crowded cities and people started to recognise the importance of hygiene. Some now bought metal bathtubs for their homes, although for most people there was no bathroom and the water still had to be carried in from outside and heated up. Many people still didn't use to have baths in their homes, but some could afford to make a weekly visit to the new public baths that opened in the 19th century. At the same time, bathing in the sea became popular as people looked to saltwater to help cure skin problems.

Bathing habits changed for good in the late 19th century when pipes could carry water directly into homes. Bathing became a lot easier and people started taking many more baths. However, many homes in the UK, especially those in rural areas, had to wait until as late as the 1960s before they had running water directly connected to them.

3 2.05 Read and listen to the article again. Mark the sentences T (true) or F (false).

1 In medieval England many people believed water was important for your health. [t]
2 Flower petals helped to keep people clean. [f]
3 King John had a bathtub made for him everywhere he went. [f]
4 Bathing in rivers was common in medieval times. [t]
5 By the early 1800s some people had hot water in their homes. [f]
6 In the early 1800s bathing in the sea was thought to help skin problems. [t]
7 Most homes in the UK had running water by the 1940s. [f]

4 SPEAKING Work in pairs. Discuss these questions.

1 How do medieval bathing habits compare with those of today?
2 How might bathing habits change in the future? Why do you think this?

GRAMMAR
would and *used to*

past simple

5 Complete these sentences from the article on page 24. Then complete the rule with *used to* / *didn't use to* and *would(n't)*.

1 King John used to take his bathtub with him whenever he travelled.
2 People … would wash using only cold water and a cloth.
3 Many people still didn't used to have baths in their homes.

> **RULE:**
> To talk about habits and repeated actions in the past, we can use ***used to* / *didn't use to*** or ***would(n't)***.
> - We use [4] used to with both action and stative verbs.
> - We use [5] would only with action verbs.

6 Choose the correct words. Sometimes both options are possible.

1 When I was a child, I *would* / *used to* play a lot with my sister.
2 We *would* / *used to* have a cat, Tubby.
3 We *would* / *used to* like her a lot and play with her all the time.
4 It's funny, but I *would* / *used to* think I'd never learn to read.
5 I *would* / *used to* sit and talk to my grandmother for hours.
6 My sister and I *would* / *used to* be such good friends!

7 Complete the sentences and conversations with the correct form of *used to*.

1 A Did you used to have a pet when you were a child?
B Yes, I used to have a cat.
2 We didn't used to have a car. We used to walk everywhere.
3 A Did you used to watch a lot of TV when you were younger?
B Yes, I used to watch it every day when I got home from school.
4 I didn't used to like vegetables, but I love them now.
5 A Did your dad used to read you stories before you went to bed?
B No, he didn't, but my mum used to.
6 I didn't used to like having birthday parties. I was a really shy child.

→ workbook page 19

VOCABULARY
Time periods

8 Look at phrases (1–9) and match them with categories (a–c).

a the present
b the recent past
c a long, long time ago in history

1 from 1995 until 2004 ☐
2 in medieval times ☐
3 in this day and age ☐
4 these days ☐
5 in the olden days ☐
6 in the last century ☐
7 nowadays ☐
8 a decade ago ☐
9 not so long ago ☐

→ workbook page 20

FUNCTIONS
Talking about the past

9 SPEAKING **Work in pairs. Choose a topic for your partner and a period in the past. Your partner makes a comparison between the present and that time period. Take turns.**

food | games | home | school | technology | travel

games in the 1930s

Well, children would play with teddy bears or dolls. These days, many children have electronic games.

Culture

TH!NK
Living in different climates

1 SPEAKING **Work in pairs. Look at the photos and try to match each one with a part of the world.**

Australia | the Himalayas | the Philippines | the Andes

2 2.06 **Read and listen to the article. Check your ideas.**

A

CREATIVE CLIMATE SOLUTIONS

Climate change is the biggest threat to our planet. As temperatures increase, the ice caps and glaciers around the world are starting to melt, meaning sea levels will get higher. We are already seeing the results of climate change with an increase in extreme weather events such as hurricanes and wildfires and serious shortages of water.

All over the world there are people living in difficult conditions. But difficult conditions often inspire creative solutions.

Every year the Philippines are hit by huge tropical typhoons. These violent storms often kill hundreds of people and cause billions of dollars in damage to the islands. In an attempt to fight back, one company has come up with a house that is designed to stand up to the strongest of winds. The houses are built in a dome shape and the curved surfaces are much better at surviving in storms than traditional flat roofs and walls. They are also better at surviving earthquakes.

Wildfires often cause massive destruction in many places around the world, destroying land, homes and lives. In 2015 bush fires burned down vegetation in a large area of South Australia leaving nothing but bare earth. This made the land difficult to farm as strong winds blew the soil away. A farmer called Brian Fischer had a brilliant idea to stop the problem. With the help of his sons he ploughed the fields in spirals. This means that it doesn't matter which way the wind blows because it can never blow away the soil.

One man who wanted to tackle global warming directly was inventor Eduardo Gold. He used the idea that light colours reflect the sunlight to try to stop mountains in the South American Andes from heating up and losing their glaciers. His plan was simple; with the help of a few friends he started painting the mountains white in the hope it would keep their surfaces cooler. Although his idea was included in the World Bank's '100 ideas to save the planet' in 2009, Gold died in 2014 and his work had limited success.

A lack of water is one of the most serious problems we can face. In the Himalayan Desert water is very difficult to find during the spring months. To help solve this problem, the Ice Stupa project has come up with a very clever solution. In winter, a pipe takes water from higher up in the mountains down to the desert, where it rushes out as a fountain. Because it is so cold in the desert, the water freezes and makes frozen towers of ice. In the spring the ice melts giving the farmers the water they need for their land.

B

C

D

3 **Read the article again. Answer the questions.**

1 What shape are the houses in the Philippines and why?
2 What caused the problem in Australia and how did one farmer try to solve it?
3 What problem does an ice stupa solve?
4 What did Eduardo Gold do and why?

4 SPEAKING **Work in pairs. What other areas of the world are difficult to live in and why?**

5 **VOCABULARY There are eight highlighted words or phrases in the article. Match the words with these meanings. Write the words.**

1 to survive by resisting ______
2 large parts of frozen land ______
3 a structure that forces water up in the air ______
4 material on the surface of the ground ______
5 to motivate ______
6 to find an answer to ______
7 something there is not enough of ______
8 to send light back ______

WRITING

A magazine article about someone who made an important discovery

1 **INPUT Read the article. What discovery did John James Audubon make?**

2 **ANALYSE Find examples in the article of:**

1 a sentence containing the past simple and the past continuous.
2 the past perfect simple.
3 the past perfect continuous.
4 expressions referring back to the past.

3 **Read the essay again and make notes to complete the table.**

	John James Audubon
His background	
What he discovered and how he discovered it	
Other information	

4 **PLAN Think of someone who made a discovery.**

- Do some internet research to find out more about them.
- Choose the most important and interesting details.
- Organise the information into paragraphs. Write notes in the table above.
- Think about the language you'll need to describe the person and what they did.

5 **PRODUCE Write an article for your school magazine about a person who made a discovery (200 words).**

John James Audubon

John James Audubon was an American bird expert and wildlife painter. He was born in 1785 in Saint-Domingue in the Caribbean. He was brought up in France, but at the age of 18 his father sent him to live in the US.

Audubon had always had a fascination for wildlife and, in particular, birdlife. He spent much of his time outdoors, studying and drawing nature. One of the things he had been wondering about was whether the same birds returned each year to his farm after disappearing for the winter months. One day, while he was drawing, he had an idea to test his theory. He caught a few birds and tied some cotton around their legs. The next year when he saw a bird with the cotton around its leg return, he knew his ideas were correct. He was one of the first people to start to understand bird migration and popularise birdwatching.

As well as his important studies into bird life, Audubon was an amazing artist. His *The Birds of America* is considered to be one of the best bird books ever written. These days it's also one of the most expensive: an original copy was recently sold for $7 million. He also identified 25 new species of birds and is regarded as a true hero of early American conservation.

READING AND USE OF ENGLISH

Multiple-choice cloze

→ workbook page 17

1 For questions 1–8, read the text below and decide which answer (A, B, C or D) best fits each gap. There is an example at the beginning (0).

0 A (stopped) B finished C ended D not

Do you ever stop and think about how easy the internet has made our lives? I know there are times when it's slow or has [0] __A__ working altogether, times when maybe you feel like [1] ______ your computer into pieces. But just think of all those things you use it for. You want to buy a new book – you can [2] ______ online and buy it. You need to [3] ______ some research for your homework – you can find it all there on the web. You feel like a [4] ______ with your best friend, so you Skype them. You just want a [5] ______ from your homework, so you start up Minecraft or whatever game it is you prefer and start playing. These [6] ______ , everything we need is just a click of a button away.

Of course, it wasn't always like this. Only a few decades [7] ______ , people had to do things like go to the shops if they wanted to buy something and often those shops were closed! They had to look in very large, heavy books called encyclopedias to find information. They had to [8] ______ up the telephone if they wanted to talk, and if their best friend wasn't at home, they simply couldn't talk to them. That's how tough life was! And these poor people who had to suffer such hardships were … our parents! Makes you feel sorry for them, doesn't it?

	A	B	C	D
1	begging	striking	forcing	smashing
2	come	enter	click	go
3	do	make	find	ask
4	talking	chat	question	speak
5	break	stop	end	fix
6	times	ages	years	days
7	after	since	ago	past
8	take	pick	grab	hold

SPEAKING

Interview

→ workbook page 25

2 In pairs, ask and answer the questions.

1 Who do you spend the most time with at the weekends, and what do you do with them?
2 What kind of films do you like best? What do you like about them?
3 Where did you go for your last holiday? What was it like?
4 What's your favourite sport to play? What do you like about it?
5 What things do you enjoy doing the most with your parents?
6 What is your favourite room in your home and why do you like it?
7 If you could be anywhere now, where would it be and why?
8 What things do you like to do at home on a rainy day?
9 Who is your best friend and what do you like the most about him/her?

VOCABULARY

1 Complete the sentences with the words in the list. There are four extra words.

~~change~~ | ~~demolished~~ | ~~do~~ | ~~forced~~ | form | ~~give up~~ | ~~got into~~ | got promoted | make | ~~retire~~ | settle | strike | struggle | travel

1 It would be wonderful to ___travel___ the world one day.
2 I'm happy I ___got into___ the habit of exercising every day.
3 He would always arrive late, and no one could make him ___change___ his ways.
4 Good luck with the test – I'm sure you'll ___do___ really well.
5 Every 31 December, I ___make___ a resolution to do something, but I usually break it!
6 Mum makes more money now because she ___got promoted___ .
7 On her 65th birthday, she decided to ___retire___ and never work again.
8 I need more time to study for my exams, so I'm going to ___give up___ my judo classes for a while.
9 The hurricane ___demolished___ more than 50 homes in the town.
10 As the flames got closer many people were ___forced___ to leave their homes.

/10

GRAMMAR

2 Complete the sentences with the phrases in the list. There are two extra phrases.

~~was looking~~ | would look | ~~'m seeing~~ | ~~are going to~~ | go to | ~~used to love~~ | ~~see~~ | ~~'ll love~~

1 I ___see~~seeing~~___ my aunt and uncle once a month.
2 Four or five of us ___are going to___ eat curry tonight.
3 Have fun at the concert – I'm sure you___'ll love___ it!
4 When I was a kid, I ___used to love___ going to the river to swim.
5 I'm not very well, so I ___'m seeing___ the doctor tomorrow.
6 When I saw her, she ___was looking___ in a shop window.

3 Find and correct the mistake in each sentence.

1 When he was young, my dad used to reading books about nature.
2 When I got to the house, there was no one there. The party finished!
3 I am running in the park every morning before school.
4 We're really excited because we will go on holiday next week.
5 He was tired because he had been running two kilometres.
6 While I was cycling in the park, I was falling off my bicycle.

/12

FUNCTIONAL LANGUAGE

4 Choose the correct words.

1 A I'm angry with Mike. He's *always* / *often* making jokes about me.
B I know. He's horrible. *I don't like* / *I'm not liking* him at all.
2 A You know, in the *past* / *olden* days, people didn't have the internet.
B I know! But *these days* / *not so long ago* we can get information so quickly!
3 A Gina and I *have* / *are having* lunch tomorrow. Why don't you come, too?
B Great – thank you! *I see* / *I'll see* you at the restaurant!
4 A No one *uses* / *is using* typewriters any more.
B Not in *nowadays* / *this day and age*, no!

/8

MY SCORE /30

22–30 | 10–21 | 0–9

3 WHAT'S IN A NAME?

OBJECTIVES

FUNCTIONS: giving advice; expressing obligation; giving recommendations, warnings and prohibitions

GRAMMAR: *(don't) have to / ought to / should(n't) / must; had better (not); can('t) / must(n't)*

VOCABULARY: making and selling; expressions with *name*

Get THINKING

Watch the video and think: do you have a favourite logo? Why do you like it?

swatch

WhatsApp

JAGUAR

ORGANIC COFFEE PRET NATURAL FOOD

READING

1 **Look at the names and logos and answer the questions.**

1 These are the names and logos of various companies. What kind of products do they offer?

Jaguar sells cars.

2 Add two more names of companies or products that are famous around the world.

2 SPEAKING **Work in pairs. Some people think the name of a brand is very important. What do you think is the reason for this?**

3 **Read the blog entry on the next page quickly. Which of the brands shown above does it mention?**

4 3.01 **Read the blog entry again and listen. Answer the questions.**

1 Why do companies think a lot about a brand name?
2 What makes a good brand name?
3 Why were each of these names chosen?
- Jaguar
- Pret A Manger
- WhatsApp

4 Why was Nova a bad name for a car in Spain?
5 Why do some teenagers choose to buy more expensive products (like clothes)?

Train to THINK

Identifying the main topic of a paragraph

Writers use a new paragraph when they want to change the topic. The opening line of a paragraph usually gives you a clue about its topic.

5 **Look at paragraphs 3 and 4. What is the topic of each paragraph? Tick (✓) two options.**

A what teenagers wear to school [ ]
B brand names are important in the teenage market [√]
C some really bad brand names [ ]
D ways to pick a brand name [√]

Brand names

1 OK, so imagine you've thought of a great idea for a product to make and sell – a game, or an app, or clothes, for example. You know you can sell millions of them, but first of all, you must give the product a name – a brand name. And that may not be as easy as you think.

2 The brand name is the thing that distinguishes your product from all others, and it's really important that it makes an impact. Businesses spend a lot of time thinking about brand names; when the name has been picked, it's very difficult to change, so companies have to get it right first time.

3 So how do you choose a name? A brand name ought to be unique, memorable and easy to understand. It should create some kind of emotional connection with people who buy the product – the target market. Some companies use the family name. When Henry Ford started making cars, he just called the company Ford. But you don't have to use a family name – you can go for an image. Staying with cars, think about the brand name Jaguar, a beautiful but dangerous wild cat. What does that say about the manufacturer's product? Some companies use wordplay. It's a common technique for naming apps, for example WhatsApp (from the English expression 'What's up'?). Others like to use foreign words because they sound special or different. For example, in Britain, in Europe and in the US there's a chain of sandwich shops with the French name Pret A Manger, which means 'ready to eat'. And what do you have to be careful about when choosing a name? Well, you shouldn't choose one that might not work in certain countries or cultures. Many years ago, a car company launched a new car that they called Nova. They thought it suggested something nice and new, but in Spanish it can be read as *no va* ('it doesn't go'). Not a good name for a car in Spain, then!

4 These days, the choice of brand name is particularly important if your product is targeted at the teenage market. Teenage consumers are perhaps more concerned with brand names and company logos than any other group. When a brand, especially a clothing brand, becomes popular with teenagers, then there's a lot of pressure to wear those clothes and have the name and/or logo visible. A teacher in an American high school said: 'I certainly see that kids are obsessed with brand names. They won't buy something that's almost identical – and cheaper – simply because they feel they must wear something with the right logo.' So if you want to get into the teenage market, you have to find a product and a brand name that works with that age group, and create some great advertisements, too.

5 Companies know that the name isn't everything – the product itself has to be good, of course – but it's an essential part of the package.

SPEAKING

6 Work in pairs. Discuss these questions.

1 Can you think of any more brand names which:
   - a use a family name?
   - b try to create an image?
   - c are in another language?

2 Have you ever bought or wanted something just because of the brand? Give examples.

'I'm so glad that we don't have to wear school uniforms any more!'

GRAMMAR
(don't) have to / ought to / should(n't) / must

1 Complete the sentences from the article on page 31. Then complete the rule with *have to, don't have to, ought to, should, shouldn't* and *must*.

1 First of all, you *must* give the product a name.
2 Companies *have to* get it right first time.
3 A brand name *ought to* be unique, memorable and easy to understand.
4 But you *don't have to* use a family name.
5 And what *do* you *have to* be careful about?
6 Well, you *shouldn't* choose a name that might not work in certain countries or cultures.

> **RULE:** We use 7 *must* or *have to* to say 'this is important or necessary'. We use 8 *don't have to* to say 'this isn't important or necessary'. We use 9 *should* or 10 *ought* to tell someone that something is a good idea. We use 11 *shouldn't* to tell someone that something isn't a good idea. (***Ought to*** isn't as frequent as ***should***. It is used mostly in writing, and the negative form is rare.)

2 Complete the conversation with the correct form of *have to*.

Mandy Mum, there's a new mobile phone out. It's brilliant. I 1 *have to* get one!
Mum No way! Your mobile phone is fine. You 2 *don't have to* buy another one.
Mandy But you know what it's like at school. Everyone 3 *has to* have the latest product!
Mum Yes, and it's terrible. Why 4 *do* you all *have to* wear the same clothes, for example?
Mandy Because it's what teenagers do. You were young once. Don't you remember?
Mum I see. And I 5 *have to* go to work to pay for all these things, right?
Mandy Oh, Mum! You 6 *don't have to* be difficult!

3 Complete the conversation with suitable modal verbs. There is often more than one possible answer.

Gill The new café is great – you 1 *have to* go there.
Jack I've heard it's a bit expensive.
Gill Yes, that's true. You 2 *don't have to* go there every day. But you 3 *should* try the cakes – they're delicious!
Jack OK. What's the place called, anyway?
Gill Can you believe it's called The Coffee Shop?!
Jack What a boring name! You 4 *don't have to* be a genius to think of that! They 5 *should* have a foreign name, like Le Café.
Gill Well, OK. But it 6 *have to* be easy to pronounce. There's a shop in town called Arighi Bianchi and no one knows how to say it.
Jack But the owner is Italian. It's his name!
Gill I guess I 7 *should* know that. Anyway, I 8 *have to* go home and do my homework for tomorrow.
Jack You 9 *shouldn't* worry about that. It's easy.
Gill Really? OK, so let's go to the cinema. There's a new film that we 10 *have to* see!

→ workbook page 28

VOCABULARY
Making and selling

4 Complete the sentences with the words.

advertisement	brand	chain	consumers
image	logo	manufacturer	products

1 They make cleaning *products*, like washing powder.
2 The prices have gone up a lot, so now *consumers* have to pay more.
3 I always buy the same *brand* of shoes – they're so comfortable.
4 It's a *chain* that has shops in every town.
5 That shop has a really funny *advertisement* on TV.
6 The Nike *logo* is a large tick.
7 When the company's director went to prison, it damaged the company's *image*.
8 If it doesn't work, send it back to the *manufacturer*.

5 SPEAKING Answer the questions. Then work in pairs and compare your answers.

Can you name …
1 three places where you find advertisements?
2 a manufacturer of mobile phones?
3 a chain of shops and a chain of restaurants?
4 one thing you always buy the same brand of?

→ workbook page 30

LISTENING

6 3.02 **Listen to Paul talking to Alexandra. What is their conversation about? Choose the correct option.**

A why it's good to have a nickname
(B) how people get their nicknames
C why some people don't like their nicknames

7 3.02 **Listen again. Mark the sentences T (true) or F (false).**

1 There are at least two shortened versions of the name Alexandra. [T]
2 Paul got the nickname Smithy because he lived in a town called Smith. [F]
3 Paul's brother liked his nickname. [F]
4 Sting got his nickname because he liked bees. [F]
5 Miley Cyrus's real name is Destiny. [T]
6 Lady Gaga got her name from a text message. [T]

GRAMMAR
had better (not)

8 Complete these sentences from the listening. Then choose the correct words to complete the rule.

1 We had better go now.
2 You had better not tell anyone at school.

RULE: We use ***had* ('*d*) *better*** to warn someone that something bad will happen if they [3] ***do* / (*don't*) *do*** something. We use ***had* ('*d*) *better not*** to warn someone that bad things will happen if they (***do***) / ***don't do*** something.

9 Complete the sentences with *had better* (*not*).

1 The bus goes in two minutes. You had better run.
2 I'll lend you my pen – but you had better not break it!
3 It's going to rain. We had better go inside.
4 You have to get up very early tomorrow, so you had better go to bed. It's 1 am.
5 You had better not eat any more sweets. You'll be sick.

→ workbook page 29

FUNCTIONS
Giving advice

10 3.03 **Put the sentences in the correct order to make two conversations. Then listen and check.**

1 [3] **Liam** Why? What's her name? ✓
[1] **Liam** What's the matter, Jo? ✓
[5] **Liam** Well, you'd better get some help – quickly! ✓
[4] **Jo** It's something like Sharita Wass Ikonor. ✓
[2] **Jo** I've got to phone someone and I've no idea how to pronounce her name. ✓

2 [3] **Bob** Well, I wrote the wrong name in my birthday card to her son. I called him Jason, not Jacob. ✓
[5] **Bob** I know. She's really cross. ✓
[1] **Bob** My sister's really angry with me. ✓
[2] **Mia** Why? ✓
[4] **Mia** You'd better not do that again! ✓

11 SPEAKING **Work in pairs. Imagine you forgot your best friend's birthday. Write a conversation using *had better* (*not*).**

SPEAKING
People and their names

12 Complete the questionnaire with 1–5 (1 = I strongly agree; 5 = I strongly disagree).

1 It's cool to have a nickname. [3]
2 I only remember the names of people I like. [5]
3 I hate it when people forget my name. [3]
4 Your name is an important part of who you are. [2]
5 I feel sorry for people who have unusual names. [4]

13 Compare your answers in small groups. Which question(s) do you agree on?

READING

1 **Can you match these American cities with their nicknames?**

1 New York [2] a The Windy City
2 Chicago [1] b The Big Apple

2 **Here are seven names of real towns. What country do you think each city town is in? Choose from the list.**

Austria | Belgium | Scotland
the Netherlands | the US (x2) | Turkey

3 3.04 **Read and listen to the article and check your answers to Exercise 2.**

HW

4 **Read the article again. Answer the questions.**

1 How did Mr Deakins choose which land to take?
2 What or who is an Accidental?
3 Why was Levi Davis's store in a good position?
4 When did the place name Hot Coffee become official?
5 What problem did the village of Lost have?
6 How did they solve this problem?
7 How did the city of Batman probably get its name?
8 Why was the mayor of Batman annoyed with Christopher Nolan?

FUNNY place names

Around the world, there are lots of names for towns and villages that sound funny in English – for example, Monster in the Netherlands, Egg in Austria and Silly in Belgium. Here are a few of my favourites.

In around 1751, George Deakins was offered some land in the US by King George II of England as payment for a debt. 'You can choose a piece of land anywhere in Western Maryland,' the king said. Mr Deakins sent two teams of engineers to find the best land, without actually working together. The two teams came back with their maps and to their surprise, they discovered they had chosen exactly the same piece of land. Mr Deakins called it, 'The Accident Tract', and that's how the town got its name. And guess what a person from Accident is called: an Accidental!

In Mississippi, in the late 1800s, you had to travel a long way to take your crops to market and to buy food and provisions. When Levi Davis built a store halfway between Natchez and Mobile, it provided a welcome break. He always offered tired travellers a good pot of hot coffee which he advertised as 'the best coffee around'. Soon his store became well known as a place to stop for hot coffee and the surrounding area became known as Hot Coffee, too. In the 1920s, the name Hot Coffee began appearing on maps. Today, you can still see the road signs to Hot Coffee, but maybe it's not really 'the best coffee around' any more.

There is a little village in Aberdeenshire, Scotland called Lost. (The name comes from the word *Lòsda* in Scottish Gaelic.) Visitors loved the name and local road signs were often stolen. In fact, the longest time a sign stayed there was for three months, and the council became so fed up with this that they decided to change the name to Lost Farm. However, the local people complained. 'We're happy with the name,' they said. 'You mustn't change it.' So the name wasn't changed and instead the council made the road signs stronger. Now people can't take the signs, but they can still have their photograph taken beside them.

The Turkish city Batman takes its name from a river and not from the comic book superhero. The river's name was probably inspired by the Bati Raman Mountain. However, there is still a connection with the Batman we've seen on the screen. In 2008, the mayor of Batman said that Christopher Nolan, the director of *The Dark Knight*, should have to pay money to the city for using the name Batman without permission. 'There is only one Batman in the world', he said. 'The American film producers used the name of our city without informing us.' Of course, Nolan didn't have to pay, though. It's true that filmmakers can't steal information and ideas, but the name Batman has been around since the character was created in 1939.

SPEAKING

5 Work in pairs. Discuss these questions.

1 Do you know how your town or city got its name?
2 What funny or unusual town names are there in your country?

GRAMMAR
can('t) / must(n't)

6 Complete these sentences from the reading. Then complete the rule with *can, can't* and *mustn't*.

1 'You ___ choose a piece of land anywhere in Western Maryland'.
2 'We're happy with the name. You ___ change it.'
3 It's true that filmmakers ___ steal information and ideas.

RULE: To talk or ask about permission, we often use the modal verb [4] ___. To say what isn't allowed, we often use [5] ___ or ___.

7 Complete the sentences with *mustn't* and the verbs. Then match them with the pictures.

be | miss | run | talk

1 You ___ so loudly!
2 I ___ late.
3 I ___ the goal!
4 You ___.

8 Rewrite the sentences using modal verbs from this unit and the pronouns in brackets. There is often more than one possible answer.

0 Diving isn't allowed. (you) *You can't dive here.*
1 It isn't necessary for us to wear uniforms. (we)
2 It's a good idea to buy a new phone. (you)
3 It's OK for you to use my laptop. (you)
4 It's necessary for them to work harder. (they)
5 Are we allowed to play here? (we)

→ workbook page 29

VOCABULARY
Expressions with *name*

9 Match the underlined expressions with the definitions.

1 Tony Hawk is a big name in skateboarding.
2 He's upset because some of the other kids call him names.
3 Jay-Z isn't his real name – it's his stage name.
4 Fish, meat, vegetables, fruit – you name it, I eat it.
5 Look! It's what's-his-name / what's-her-name.
6 We want to get married, but we haven't named the day yet.
7 I know you don't want to do the exams, but it's the name of the game for university entry.
8 He made a name for himself as a great actor.

a decide the date of an event, often a wedding
b someone whose name I can't remember
c something necessary that you have to accept
d a person who is important or famous in their profession
e a name that an actor or musician uses in their profession
f use rude names about, or to, a person
g become known or respected by many people
h anything you say (or choose)

10 Complete the missing word(s).

1 She's been to Europe, Asia and Australia – you ___ ___, she's been there!
2 Hard work is the ___ of ___ ___ if you want to do well in your exams.
3 My uncle's a doctor. He's a ___ ___ in the field of cancer research.
4 Some of her classmates ___ her ___. It's horrible for her.
5 You're engaged? That's wonderful! When are you going to ___ ___ day?
6 Oh look! There's ___-his-___ – you know, that boy who lives in your street.
7 She made a ___ for ___ on a reality TV show and became a famous singer.
8 Bruno Mars is the ___ name of Pete Gene Hernandez.

→ workbook page 30

PRONUNCIATION
Strong and weak forms: /ɒv/ and /əv/
Go to page 120.

Fiction

1 Read the introduction. What kind of story is this?

How I Met Myself

by David A. Hill

John Taylor is an Englishman living in Budapest with his wife and daughter. One day he is knocked over in the street by a man who looks exactly like him – his 'doppelgänger'. He starts to look for more information about the man, and learns that he is a Hungarian called János Szabó. But he also learns that Szabo died in the 1956 Hungarian Revolution.

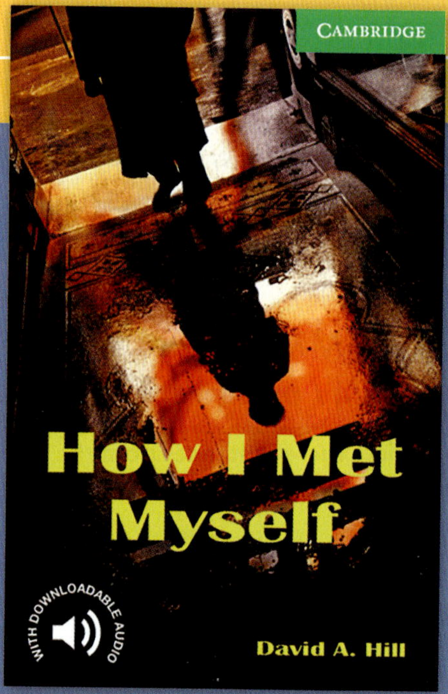

2 3.07 Read and listen to the extract. What does the Hungarian word *szabó* mean in English? Why is this important for John?

The next day, I was walking home from work. […] As I went along a street I saw some men putting up a new sign on an old shop. There was the owner's name in red, and below it the word *szabó* in green. In the window there were suits, jackets and trousers. *Szabó*. Tailor. The tailor's was getting a new sign. '*Szabó*,' I thought. Then I said 'János Szabó' out loud. Then I thought, 'Janos the tailor. John the tailor. John Taylor.' I stopped in the street. János Szabó was John Taylor! My doppelgänger and I shared a name. John Taylor was the English for the Hungarian János Szabó. My hair stood up. Here was something new and important: we shared the same name!

I […] thought about what I had discovered. I tried to decide what to do. Should I tell Andrea about this? Perhaps it would help her to believe me? I didn't know. […] I decided to go and see Mrs Fischer again. I walked quickly round to […] her flat.

'Do you remember I came to ask you about János Szabó, Mrs Fischer?' I asked when she let me in.

'Oh, the poor young man,' she said, looking at me sadly. 'And do you know something – you look so like him, too.'

This was quite a surprise. 'Really?' I asked.

'Come here under the light,' she said.

I moved under the strong light in the hall.

'Yes,' she said, looking at me carefully. 'You look very much the same. The eyes, the nose, the mouth. Very much the same. I didn't look at you carefully when you came last time. Oh, the poor young man.'

I felt myself getting very hot.

'Mrs Fischer, I came to ask you something different,' I said. Then I went on very slowly, because I was so afraid of her possible answer. 'Can you remember the names of the wife and daughter who were killed in the cellar?'

'Well, I know the wife was called Andrea,' she started, and I felt my face go white, 'but as for the little girl … let's think …'

I waited for a moment. She didn't seem able to remember.

'It wasn't …' I waited, and then said, 'It wasn't Kati, was it?'

Mrs Fischer looked at me and smiled. 'Yes, that was it,' she said. 'Quite right. Andrea and Kati. The poor young things.'

I thanked her and left as quickly as I could. My head was turning round and round. I felt sick. Outside in the cold street, I stood against the wall of the building. There were too many new things inside my head to understand at once: my doppelgänger had the same name as me – Szabó, or Taylor – I looked like him, and his wife and daughter had the same names as mine!

3 **Read the extract again. Mark the statements T (true) or F (false).**

1 John Taylor goes into a shop to buy a suit. [F]
2 He realises that János Szabó is a translation of John Taylor. [T]
3 John's wife Andrea doesn't believe something he told her. [T]
4 It is not the first time he has talked to Mrs Fischer. [T]
5 He is scared to ask Mrs Fischer about the wife and daughter's names. [T]
6 He is happy when he leaves Mrs Fischer's flat. [F]

4 SPEAKING **Work in pairs. Discuss these questions.**

1 Why does Mrs Fischer call Szabó 'the poor young man'?
2 What do you think happened in the cellar?
3 What might happen next to solve this mystery?
4 Would you like to meet someone who looks exactly like you and has the same name? Why or why not?

WRITING
A reply to a letter asking for advice

1 INPUT **Read the letter and the reply. Then answer the questions.**

1 What is Alan's problem?
2 What question does Susannah suggest that Alan asks himself?

2 **Complete the missing words from Susannah's reply.**

1 This is the first question you ______ ______ ask yourself.
2 If the answer is no, then maybe ______ ______ end the friendship now.
3 … you ______ ______ talk to him about the name-calling …
4 … and explain that he ______ ______ stop saying those things.
5 Finally, ______ ______ ______ ______ to talk to your parents.

3 ANALYSE **Read Susannah's reply again. In which paragraph does she …**

1 offer advice to make the friendship work?
2 outline Alan's problem?
3 tell him to speak to others about his problem?
4 ask Alan to think more carefully about the situation?

4 PLAN **Read another letter to Susannah. Write three pieces of advice for Lara.**

5 PRODUCE **Write a reply to Lara (150–200 words). Say what you think she should do.**

SUSANNAH'S
ADVICE PAGE

Write with your problem and Susannah will give you advice. This week's letter is from Alan in Salisbury, UK.

Dear Susannah,

Last month, we moved to a new town. My parents quickly made friends with the people who live next door. They've got a son of about my age. He's friendly and invites me to do things with him. But the thing is, when we see other kids, he calls them names and makes horrible comments. He wants me to join in, but I don't want to.

What can I do? If I tell my parents, it'll be hard because they really like his parents. And to be honest, I haven't got many other friends yet. If I stop hanging out with him, maybe he'll start calling me names, too.

What should I do?

Alan, Salisbury

Dear Alan,

It's often difficult to make new friends when you move to a new town, so it was almost perfect that your new neighbours had a son your age and that he wanted to be your friend. What a shame that you're finding it difficult to spend time with him.

You don't say in your letter if you think you could be friends if his behaviour was better. This is the first question you ought to ask yourself. If the answer is no, then maybe you'd better end the friendship now. Don't worry – I'm sure you'll soon make lots of friends when you start school.

However, if you think you could be friends, then you should definitely talk to him about the name-calling and explain that he had better stop saying those things. If he's going to be a good friend, he'll listen to you. If he ignores you, then this friendship probably isn't going to work.

Finally, it's a good idea to talk to your parents. They're the people who know you best and are often the best people to give you advice.

Good luck!

Susannah

Dear Susannah,

I have very bad eyesight and need to wear glasses. Because of this, some people at school call me names. I tried not to let it bother me too much, but the problem is that it happens quite often. I've always enjoyed school and had lots of friends, but I'm starting to hate going there. My grades are also getting worse and some of the teachers have said they're disappointed with me. I know I should talk to the teachers, but I'm sure this is only going to make things worse. Can you help?

Lara, Ipswich

4 WHAT WOULD YOU DO?

OBJECTIVES

FUNCTIONS:
talking about hypothetical situations; expressing wishes; apologising and accepting apologies

GRAMMAR:
first and second conditional (review); time conjunctions; *wish* and *if only*; third conditional (review)

VOCABULARY:
being honest; making a decision; *now*

Get THINKING

Watch the video and think: are you always honest with your friends?

A

C

B

D

READING

1 **Read the definition. Then look at the pictures. What dilemmas do you think they show?**

> **dilemma:** a situation in which a difficult choice has to be made between two or more alternatives

2 **Read the quiz on the next page quickly. Match each picture with a question.**

3 4.01 **Read and listen to the quiz. Then take the quiz and compare with a partner.**

4 **Match these responses with the quiz questions.**

a I'd keep quiet and run back to the middle of the pitch. 3
b I'd ask if I could change it for another one. 2
c I wouldn't look because I'd be scared of getting caught. 5
d I'd tell the person who did it that they should tell the truth. 6
e I'd put it in my pocket as quickly as I could. 1
f I'd make the door dirty to try and cover it up. 4

HOW HONEST ARE YOU?

Take our quiz! For each question choose A, B or C.

What would you do if …

1 you gave a £10 note to buy a £5 item, but the assistant gave you £15 change by mistake?

A I'd take the money and walk out quickly.
B I'd tell the assistant he had made a mistake and give ten pounds back.
C I'd take the money and give it to a homeless person.

2 your grandparents gave you a shirt as a present, but you didn't like it?

A I'd say thank you but never wear the shirt.
B I'd say thank you but tell them it really wasn't my style.
C I'd say thank you but only wear it when I was with them.

3 you scored a goal in a football match, but you knew it wasn't legal because the ball had hit your hand without the referee seeing it?

A I'd celebrate my goal in the usual way.
B I'd tell the referee that the ball hit my hand, so it wasn't a goal.
C I'd say sorry to the players on the other team but tell them it was the referee's mistake, not mine.

4 you kicked a stone outside your house and it made a dent in the neighbour's car door?

A I wouldn't do anything.
B I'd ring my neighbour's doorbell and tell them I'd damaged their car.
C I'd tell the neighbours that their car was damaged but I didn't know who did it.

5 you couldn't answer a question in a test, but you realised you could see another student's answer?

A I'd try to copy their answer.
B I wouldn't look, but would just try to answer the question myself.
C I'd look a little bit to help myself think more clearly.

6 your school principal wanted to know who broke a classroom window, and you knew who the person was?

A I wouldn't say anything.
B I'd go to the principal's office and say who did it.
C I'd write a note to the principal, saying who did it but without putting my name on the note.

RESULTS

MOSTLY A: Sometimes you take the easy way out. Be careful, because it may cause you problems. You don't want people to think of you as dishonest.

MOSTLY B: You're basically an honest person. You understand that if you always tell the truth, people will trust you. But don't forget that the truth can hurt a little, too, sometimes!

MOSTLY C: Perhaps you should ask yourself why you are taking this middle path between being dishonest and being completely honest? Perhaps you'd feel better if you always acted 100% honestly.

Train to THINK

Thinking of consequences

In order to make a good decision, it's important to think of all the possible consequences for others and for yourself.

5 **Choose four of the questions in the quiz. Think of possible consequences for each option.**

Question	Action	Consequence
1	*I tell the man about his mistake.*	*I don't get an extra £10.*
	I take the money.	*Maybe the man loses that money from his wages that week.*

SPEAKING

6 **Work in pairs. Discuss these questions.**

1 Which of the situations in the quiz is the most / least serious?
2 Do you agree with what the results say about you?

GRAMMAR
First and second conditional (review)

1 Complete these sentences from the quiz on page 39 with the correct forms of the verbs. Then match them with the parts of the rule.

1 What ______ you ______ (do) if you ______ (kick) a stone and it ______ (make) a dent in the neighbour's car door?

2 If you always ______ (tell) the truth, people ______ (trust) you.

> **RULE:**
> We use the first conditional to talk about real situations and their consequences. We form it with *if* + present simple / future (*will*) clause. ☐
> We use the second conditional to talk about hypothetical or very unlikely situations and their outcomes. We form it with *if* + past simple / (*would*) clause. ☐

2 Complete the conditional sentences with the correct forms of the verbs. Think carefully about whether each one is a first or second conditional.

What should I do?

Why is Jan so mean to me? If Jan [1] ______ (not be) so mean to me, I [2] ______ (want) to invite her to my party. The problem is, she's so popular. If she [3] ______ (not have) so many friends, nobody [4] ______ (care) if she was at my party or not. I have to invite her. If I [5] ______ (not invite) Jan to my party, nobody [6] ______ (come) to it. Maybe I shouldn't have a party. But if I [7] ______ (not have) a party, I [8] ______ (not get) any presents and I want presents! Why are birthdays always so much trouble? If it [9] ______ (not be) my birthday next week, my life [10] ______ (not be) so complicated. If I [11] ______ (know) what to do, I [12] ______ (do) it. But I don't!

→ workbook page 36

Time conjunctions

3 Complete the sentences with the words.

as soon as | if | unless | until | when

1 I don't know where he is, but I'll tell him ______ I see him.
2 I'm meeting him later, so I'll tell him ______ I see him.
3 It's really important. I'm going to tell him ______ I see him.
4 I won't tell him anything ______ he asks.
5 I'll work ______ he arrives and then I'll stop.

4 Complete the sentences so that they are true for you. Tell your partner.

1 As soon as I get home tonight, I …
2 If the weather is good this weekend, I …
3 When I'm 18, I …
4 Unless I get lots of homework this weekend, I …
5 I'm going to save all my money until …

→ workbook page 36

VOCABULARY
Being honest

5 Write the words in the correct columns.

cheat | get away with something | hide the truth | do the right thing | tell a lie | be open about something | tell the truth | own up to something

Positive behaviour	Negative behaviour
	cheat

6 Compete the conversation with the correct form of the verbs from Exercise 5.

Dan I've got a dilemma. The other day I [1] ______ in a test. I copied from Ben.

Ana Why?

Dan Well, I thought I could [2] ______ away with it, but now the teacher wants to know who copied who. I said it was Ben.

Ana You should [3] ______ up to it and say it was you.

Dan I know, but it's too difficult to [4] ______ the truth.

Ana But you can't [5] ______ the truth now! What about poor Ben? What were you thinking?

Dan It's Maths. I just find it so difficult.

Ana Well, you need to [6] ______ about this. First, say sorry for cheating and explain why you [7] ______ a lie. Then tell your teacher what the problem is.

Dan You're right, of course. It's just so difficult to [8] ______ the right thing sometimes.

→ workbook page 38

LISTENING

7 SPEAKING **Work in pairs. Look at the photo. What do you think they are doing?**

8 4.02 **Listen to the conversation. Were you right? What did they decide to do?**

9 4.02 **Listen again. Choose the correct answers.**

1 Why are the teenagers there?
- **A** they are going on a long journey
- **B** they are waiting for a friend
- **C** they are going home

2 What do they decide to play?
- **A** a card game invented by Angie
- **B** a guessing game invented by Stuart
- **C** a traditional children's game

3 Why does Maria say 'a cartoon animal, perhaps'?
- **A** because animals aren't usually tall
- **B** because the game can only have fictional characters
- **C** because Stuart is thinking of a non-human character

4 Why does Angie give three clues at the same time?
- **A** because Jenny's bus is arriving
- **B** because she wants to make the game easier
- **C** because she's bored with the game

5 Why is Angie wrong to make Gru say,'I wish I could steal the moon'?
- **A** because in the film, Gru steals the moon
- **B** because in the film, Gru doesn't steal the moon
- **C** because Angie is reading *The Lord of the Rings*

GRAMMAR
wish and *if only*

10 Read the sentences. Which fictional characters might say them? Complete the rule. Use the sentences to help you.

1 'If only I **spoke** Luke Skywalker's language.'
2 'I wish I **could** get the ring back.'
3 'I wish those three girls **would** go to sleep.'

RULE:
- We use *wish / if only* + the [4] past simple tense to express how we would like our current situation to be different.
- We use *wish / if only* + [5] could to say that we'd like the ability to do something.
- We use *wish / if only* + [6] would to say that we'd like something to happen or someone (else) to do something.

Look

We can use *was* or *were* after a singular subject (*I, he, she* or *it*) when we express wishes.

I wish I was older. / I wish I were older.

11 Complete the sentences with the correct forms of the verbs.

be | go | have | knock | like | not have

1 I wish I were taller.
2 I wish you liked me more.
3 If only I had a more interesting book to read.
4 I wish I didn't have this awful headache.
5 If only I could go to sleep.
6 I wish you knocked before you come into my room!

12 SPEAKING **Play 'famous wishes' in groups of four.**

- Choose a famous fictional person and write three wishes.
  (Remember: they should be about the present situation, not the past.)
- Read out your sentences. The other students have to guess who you are.

→ workbook page 37

READING

1 4.03 **Read and listen to the stories. Match the stories (1–3) with the pictures (A–C).**

2 **Read the stories again. Who do you think said these things?**

1 'I found this in your bin.'
2 'I was very surprised when I read the letter.'
3 'They let you out too soon.'
4 'It's incredible that you brought it back to us.'
5 'OK, you can go now.'
6 'It was a long time ago, but I've always been sorry for what I did.'

3 SPEAKING **Work in pairs. Decide what you would have done in each situation. Then compare with other students.**

HOW HONEST IS THAT?

1 MAKING IT RIGHT – MANY YEARS LATER

The manager of a shop in Seattle was very surprised one day in 2011 when a man came in, gave him an envelope and left. The manager opened the envelope and found a $100 note and a short letter. The letter said: 'I stole $25 from this store in 1961. Now that I've got some money, I want to give it back. If you had put it in the bank, it would have grown to $100. So here it is.'
The newspapers wanted to know who the man was, but the manager didn't release his name.

2 BACK TO PRISON

In 2011, Luis Lopez was sent to prison in Florida for a year. After three months, the prison guards came and told him he could go home. Amazed, Lopez asked the guards if they were sure – they said yes, so he left. But it didn't feel right to Lopez, so when he got home, he called his lawyer. The lawyer told him that in fact the local court had made a mistake. He advised Lopez to go back and finish his prison sentence – and that's what he did. If he hadn't gone back to prison, he would have had bigger problems.

3 A LITTLE MONEY, A LOT OF HONESTY

Now and again, people throw things away by mistake. One day, rubbish collector Jimmy James found a $50 store gift card amongst the rubbish outside a home. He went on working, but later that day, Jimmy went back to the house, rang the doorbell and gave the family the card. They were very surprised because $50 didn't seem like a lot of money to them. But Jimmy just said he thought it was the right thing to do. The family gave him a $75 reward to say thank you.

A 2

B 1

C 3

GRAMMAR
Third conditional (review)

4 **Complete these sentences from the story with the correct forms of the verbs. Then complete the rule.**

1 If Lopez hadn't gone (not go) back to prison, he would have (have) bigger problems.
2 If you had put (put) it in the bank, it would have grown (grow) to $100.

RULE:
We use the third conditional to talk about imagined situations and their outcomes in the past. We form it with:
if + ³ past perfect + *would(n't) have* + ⁴ P. participle

5 **Complete the third conditional sentences.**

0 If the court ***hadn't made*** a mistake, Lopez ***wouldn't have left*** prison early.
1 If the store hadn't release (release) the video, everyone would have known (know) the man's name.
2 If Jimmy James had kept (keep) the card, he wouldn't have got (not get) the reward.

6 **Complete the sentences so that they are true for you.**

1 If I hadn't gone to school today, I wouldn't ...
2 I'd have been really happy if I was on holiday yet.
3 If I'd been born 100 years ago, I would ...

→ workbook page 37

VOCABULARY
Making a decision

7 Match a–h with the underlined words and phrases in the text below.

a for a long time	2	**e** make	8
b a good	4	**f** thought again about	5
c a bad	7	**g** original idea	1
d decide	6	**h** made a new decision	3

My [1]first thought was to go with the blue. But then I thought [2]long and hard and [3]changed my mind. Maybe the red was better. But had I made [4]the right decision? Had I? I [5]reconsidered my choice. Red or blue? Red or blue? Why was it so difficult to [6]make up my mind? Well, I didn't want to make [7]the wrong decision, did I? So I called my sister. Maybe she could help me [8]come to a decision.

'I don't know why you're asking me,' she said. 'You only ever wear blue.'

8 SPEAKING **Work in pairs. Discuss these questions.**

1 What's the biggest decision you've ever made?
2 Have you ever made the wrong decision? What was it?
3 How good are you at making your mind up about small things?
4 What sort of things do you usually need to think long and hard about?
5 Do you ever reconsider decisions you've made?
6 Who do you ask to help you come to important decisions?

→ workbook page 38

WordWise: Phrases with *now*

9 Look at the words and phrases in bold in these sentences from the unit. Match them with the definitions.

1 OK, you can go **now**.
2 **Now that** I've got some money, I want to give it back.
3 **Now and again**, people throw things away by mistake.
4 I looked at the station sign **just now**, but it doesn't say.
5 Do you want to have a go **now**, Angie?

5 **a** in the near future
1 **b** at this moment
4 **c** a moment or two ago
2 **d** because finally
3 **e** sometimes

10 Use words and phrases from Exercise 9 to complete the sentences.

1 I've finished my work, so __5__ I'm going to hang out with my friends.
2 I don't listen to this music all the time, but __3__ I like to play it.
3 Sally was here __4__, but she's gone out.
4 I'll eat later. I'm not hungry __1__.
5 I don't walk to school __2__ I've got a bike.

→ workbook page 38

TH!NK values
Doing the right thing

11 Think about a time when you had to make a difficult decision. Make notes.

1 What decision did you make?
2 What were the consequences?

12 Write a short paragraph. Include a third conditional sentence.

Last year, there was a new student in my class. Nobody wanted to sit next to him, so I did. I'm really happy I did. If I hadn't sat next to him, he wouldn't have become my best friend. What a good decision I made!

13 Read your paragraph out to the class. Then vote on the best story.

WRITING
A diary entry about a dilemma

14 Choose one of these situations or use your own idea. Write a diary entry about it (150–200 words). Try to use language from this unit.

1 Explain the problem.
2 Think about two possible solutions and their consequences.
3 Decide what you're going to do and why.

- You've got a detention. If you tell your parents, you won't be allowed to go to a party.
- It's your mum's birthday this weekend, but you spent all your money on clothes and haven't got any left to buy her a present.
- You saw your best friend's boyfriend / girlfriend at the cinema with another boy / girl.

1 4.04 **Look at the photo. Who do you think the two people are and what are they talking about? Listen and read to check.**

Dad: What's with the worried face, Tom?
Tom: Well, I'm thinking about what to study if I go to university.
Dad: Well, I'd like to help if I can. Any chance?
Tom: Of course, Dad! Believe it or not, I really like it when we talk together.
Dad: Well, me too. OK, so if I remember rightly, you're torn between doing Spanish or Economics.
Tom: Exactly. And between you and me, I'm pretty good at both. They just seem to lead in different directions.
Dad: How do you mean?
Tom: Well, if I carry on with Economics, I think I'll end up in an office job. But do I want that?
Dad: And Spanish?
Tom: Well, then I could live in a Spanish-speaking country, like Peru or Ecuador, and that could be exciting. But do I want to live so far away? And what job would I do? Teaching? I don't know. It's a dilemma.
Dad: Listen, don't overthink it. There's no hurry. You've got six months before you have to choose. And if you still can't decide – well, just go with your instinct.
Tom: Thanks, Dad. I'll do that. Can we keep talking about this?
Dad: Of course. Now Tom, I was wondering if you could help me with a dilemma. Should I cook dinner or should I ask you to?
Tom: Dad! Are you out of your mind? You're a hopeless cook! I'll do it!

2 4.04 **Read and listen to the dialogue again. Answer the questions.**

1 What is Tom's dilemma?
2 What are his worries about doing Economics?
3 What are his worries about doing Spanish?
4 What does he think of his father's cooking?

3 SPEAKING **Discuss the statements in pairs. What do you think?**

1 Tom's dilemma is an important one.
2 Tom should probably choose Spanish because then he can travel.
3 His father gives him good advice.

Phrases for fluency

4 **Find the underlined expressions in the dialogue. How do you say them in your language? Use the expressions to complete the mini-dialogues.**

1 A Andy, I was wondering if you could come and help me choose my next tattoo?
B Sorry, no. Between you and me, I don't think tattoos look good on you at all.
2 A Hi, Steve. Wow! What's with those really old football boots?
B They're ancient, aren't they? Believe it or not, my dad used to wear them when he was at school. I need new ones.
3 A Listen, Jane. I love that new necklace of yours. Any chance I could borrow it tonight?
B Are you out of your mind? It's really expensive! I wouldn't lend it to anyone!

FUNCTIONS
Apologising and accepting apologies

KEY LANGUAGE

No problem.	I feel awful about this.
That's / It's OK.	I don't know what to say.
Don't worry about it.	No worries.
I'm so ashamed.	I'm so sorry.

5 **Write the expressions from the Key Language box in the correct columns.**

Apologising	Accepting apologies

6 SPEAKING **Work in pairs. Imagine you're in these situations and act out conversations. Use expressions from the Key Language box.**

- A has spilled a drink on B's trousers.
- A has arrived very late for a meeting with B.
- A has bumped into B and B has fallen over.
- A has completely forgotten B's name.

PRONUNCIATION
Consonant–vowel word linking Go to page 120.

LIFE COMPETENCIES

We all act on instinct at some point in our lives, and acting on instinct can have positive or negative consequences.

1 ▶ 11 **Watch the vlog. What is Serena's dilemma?**

2 ▶ 11 **Watch the vlog again and answer the questions.**

1 What are the bad things about Mandy?
2 What are the good things about Nadia?
3 What did Serena do with the kitten on the street?
4 What happened with the cake in the fridge?
5 What is Serena's final decision?

3 Read the start of Marta's story. What do you think she should do?

In the summer holidays my friends and I met up for a picnic and a game of football. We had a great day, the weather was good and we all had fun. My friend Ellie needed to be home by 9 pm and by this time it was getting dark. The cycle ride back to her house takes her along a quiet footpath in the woods and across a main road. Ellie was happy to walk back to her house by herself, but I felt worried about her.

TIPS FOR ACTING ON INSTINCT

- **If something doesn't feel right, take some more time to think about it.** conditional 0
- **If your friends are all doing one thing but you feel it isn't right, don't feel pressured into behaving in a way you don't agree with. If your instinct says no, don't do it.** conditional 0
- **Acting on instinct can be a good thing. If you think your actions will benefit or help someone else, go ahead and do what you feel!** conditional 0

you use it to give advise

4 Now read endings A and B. What was the result of Marta's actions in each ending?

A

It was nearly dark; what if she met a stranger in the woods or got lost? I said I would walk with her, and then we would call my dad from her house to pick me up. At first, Ellie said she was fine, she didn't want me to have to call my dad. But when I insisted I was worried about her, finally she agreed and we both got home safely.

B

It was getting dark, but I thought she'd think I was being silly if I told her how I felt. I asked her to text me when she got home. At 10 pm Ellie's mum called me. She was at the hospital with Ellie. On her way home, she had twisted her ankle, and couldn't walk on it. Because she was on her own, she had been frightened and upset, but she had managed to call her mum on her mobile phone.

5 Answer the questions about the story.

1 How would you have acted in the situation?
2 What was Marta's instinct in ending A?
3 How do you think Marta feels in ending B?

Me and my world

6 SPEAKING **Work in pairs. What is your instinct in each of the situations? Would you normally act on your instinct? Why or why not?**

A You are at the local skate park. Your friend is about to do a dangerous jump. He's not wearing a helmet.

B You are with a group of friends. A few of them are being unkind to another friend in your group.

C You have always wanted to buy a particular thing but it's very expensive. One day you see it in a sale, 40% off the original price – but it's still more than you can really afford. Your friend offers to lend you the money to buy it.

TOWARDS B2 First for Schools

LISTENING
Multiple choice

→ workbook page 35

1 4.07 **You will hear people talking in eight different situations. For questions 1–8, choose the best answer (A, B or C).**

1 You hear a boy talking about how he got his name. Why was it hard for his parents to name him?
A They each wanted different names.
B There weren't many possibilities for a name that worked in two languages.
C He was born two weeks early.

2 You hear a girl talking on her phone. What is her problem?
A She doesn't want to invite Lucy to her birthday celebration.
B Her mum said that Lucy can't come for a sleepover.
C She really wants to have a big party.

3 You hear part of an interview with a footballer. What does he find most difficult about his job?
A not being free at weekends
B having to work out every day
C the comments some of the fans make

4 You hear two friends talking about a camping trip. What advice does Alan give Steve?
A to take a comfortable sleeping bag
B to get a lift to the campsite
C not to take things that weigh too much

5 You hear a local news report. What did Clive Roberts think when he found the money?
A I'm £10,000 richer.
B How can I return this to the owner?
C Could I keep this? Would anybody ever know?

6 Two friends are talking about a party. Why did Chloë miss the party?
A Her dad said she had to go cycling with him.
B She fell asleep in the middle of the day.
C She was watching TV and forgot the time.

7 You hear a girl talking about a difficult decision. Why did she find it hard to choose which exams to take?
A She had no idea about what career she wanted to do.
B She didn't want to disappoint her dad.
C She wanted to make sure her exams would help her get a well-paid job.

8 You hear a book review on the radio. What did Carla like best about the book?
A that she was able to understand the story
B that it was a love story
C the way the characters developed during the story

8

WRITING
Story

→ workbook page 43

2 **Your English teacher has asked you to write a short story for the school's new website. The story must begin or end with the following words:**

I still don't know why I didn't tell the truth.

Write your story in 140–190 words.

VOCABULARY

1 Complete the sentences with the words / phrases in the list. There are four extra words / phrases.

brand | call | chain | cheat | consumers | get away with | image | logo
manufacturer | make | name | own up to | products | tell

1 He worked hard for a long time before he started to ______ a name for himself in cinema.
2 The company was in trouble until they started making some new ______ .
3 If you ______ during the exam, we'll take you out of the exam room and destroy your paper.
4 I like so many different kinds of fruit. Basically, you ______ it, I like it!
5 He tried to look at another boy's test, but the teacher saw him so he didn't ______ it.
6 Other kids used to ______ me names, but it never upset me.
7 Our website has been redesigned – and if you visit it, you'll see that we have a new ______ , too.
8 It's not always easy, but it's important always to ______ the truth.
9 We started with just one shop, but now we have a ______ of 20.
10 I know you took my things without asking. Why don't you just ______ it?

/10

GRAMMAR

2 Complete the sentences with the words in the list. There are two extra words.

better | go | if | ought | unless | until | went | when

1 It's pretty late – I think I have to ______ now, OK?
2 I really wish we ______ out to eat more often.
3 I'll call you ______ the film finishes, OK?
4 I'm not going to bed ______ I finish this book – it's brilliant!
5 You'll never be his friend ______ you go and talk to him!
6 It's a secret, so you'd ______ not tell anyone else!

3 Find and correct the mistake in each sentence.

1 You shouldn't to talk to a teacher like that. It isn't respectful.
2 If they wouldn't be so expensive, I'd buy those trainers.
3 I wish you don't live so far away.
4 Your eye looks bad – I think you better go to the doctor.
5 If it hadn't rained, we had gone for a walk yesterday.
6 If only we can see you more often.

/12

FUNCTIONAL LANGUAGE

4 Choose the correct words.

1 A I think we *should* / *ought* to go now.
B That's a shame. If only you *could stay* / *stayed* a little longer.
2 A Listen, we *mustn't* / *don't have to* miss the last bus tonight.
B You're right. *I'd better not* / *I don't have to* forget to set an alarm on my phone.
3 A Sorry, but you *don't* / *can't* come in. You're too young!
B I know. But I really want to see the film. I wish I *would be* / *were* 18 already!
4 A Patrick *wouldn't have* / *won't have* come to the party if he'd known Sue was going to be there.
B Yeah, it's a shame – if only *we'd told* / *we've told* him earlier.

/8

MY SCORE /30

22–30 | 10–21 | 0–9

5 STORYTELLING

OBJECTIVES

FUNCTIONS:
telling a story

GRAMMAR:
relative pronouns; defining and non-defining relative clauses; relative clauses with *which*

VOCABULARY:
elements of a story; types of story

Get THINKING

Watch the video and think: what makes a really good story?

READING

1 SPEAKING **Think of an example of each of these things. Then work in pairs and share one or two of your ideas.**

- a story or a favourite fairy tale from your childhood
- a favourite film
- a thriller (either a book or a film) that really grabbed you
- an anecdote or a joke you've heard recently

2 SPEAKING **What are the ingredients of a good story? Discuss with a partner. Then compare your ideas with the rest of the class.**

3 5.01 **Read and listen to the article on the next page. Were your ideas the same as the writer's?**

4 **Choose the correct answers to the questions.**

1 What advice does the writer give about getting started?
A Think carefully about how all the events in the story will develop.
B Choose your best idea and just start writing.
C Write the first thing that comes into your head.

2 What does the writer say is important for a good plot?
A a happy ending
B a fight between good and bad
C a situation where there is conflict

3 What does the writer suggest about the theme of a novel?
A You should try to make it as clever as possible.
B It is more important than your plot.
C Your reader should work it out for themselves.

4 What does the writer suggest about the characters?
A Get to know them as you write.
B Make sure you tell your reader exactly what they look like.
C Let them make mistakes.

5 What advice does he give about writing style?
A Keep your reader in mind.
B Take your time to think of the right words.
C Try to copy the style that other writers use.

SO YOU WANT TO WRITE A NOVEL, DO YOU?

About Blog Latest posts Archives

What's stopping you? Time? Ideas? Self-belief? Well, let me help you. Time: find half an hour to write every day. You'll be surprised to see how quickly the pages start filling up. Ideas: write down loads and then choose the best. You only need one main idea. Start writing and the rest will soon come. Self-belief: what can I say? You can do it. I know you can. Remember, your novel, which will be fun to write, doesn't need to be 600 pages long. You could start with a short one.

What else do you need to know? Here are a few rules I always follow that might help you:

I always like to start with the plot. That's because I like a novel with a good story. And a good story comes from conflict. Many of the best novels start in a good place where the main character is happy with their life. Then something goes wrong and as the situation gets worse, our hero is thrown into conflict. The plot is then driven by how they can make things better. But in their struggle to right these wrongs the character should learn something about themselves.

The theme, which is basically the message that the story is trying to get across, is also important. This is something you should never tell your reader directly. No one likes to be told what's right or what's wrong. The best thing to do is to let your reader work out the message on their own. That way your novel will make them feel clever and they'll want to read your next one!

Characters. They're important! Before you start writing, get to know the people whose stories you will be telling. Ask yourself questions about them. Get inside their heads and answer your questions. Don't spend too much time describing what they look like. What's important is what they're like inside. Who are they? What motivates them? Why are they doing those things? And they shouldn't be perfect. They're humans (presumably). They need to make mistakes from time to time, and as they try to deal with the conflict in their life, they should develop and change.

Finally, you might want to think about your own writing style – the words you are going to use to write your story. You don't need to use long complex sentences or words that will leave your readers confused (but some variety in words is good!). You can keep your style simple. Think about the people who might want to read your story. Think about how to keep them interested. But be yourself. Write the words that come most naturally. These will always be your best words. So there you have it: plot, theme, characters and style. Follow these golden rules and you'll never go wrong. Of course, though, don't forget – rules are often there to be broken.

Train to TH!NK

Thinking about different writing styles

Writers use different techniques to bring their texts alive.

5 Answer the questions.

1 What technique does the writer use in the title of the article?
2 How many times does he use this technique in the article?
3 Why do you think he does this?

6 Choose the correct option.

1 When people ask a rhetorical question, they …
A expect an answer.
B don't really expect an answer.
2 They ask a rhetorical question to …
A introduce a subject they want to talk about.
B find out what you're thinking.

7 Some of the paragraphs don't contain any rhetorical questions. Think of a rhetorical question that you could add to the final paragraph.

SPEAKING

8 Work in pairs. Discuss these questions.

1 What kind of stories do you enjoy most? Give an example.
2 What kind of story would you like to write most?

Grammar rap!

GRAMMAR
Relative pronouns

1 Complete these sentences from the article on page 49. Then complete the rule.

1 Think about the people who might want to read your story.
2 Get to know the people whose stories you will be telling.
3 The theme, which is basically the message that the story is trying to get across, is also important.
4 Many of the best novels start in a good place where the main character is happy with their life.

> **RULE:**
> We use relative clauses to give extra information. We use …
> 5 who to refer to people.
> 6 which and that to refer to things.
> 7 whose to refer to possessions.
> 8 where to refer to places.

2 Combine the sentences by replacing the underlined words with relative pronouns from Exercise 1.

1 One of the world's greatest storytellers was Roald Dahl. <u>He</u> wrote wonderful books for children.
2 Many people love his children's stories. <u>The children's stories</u> are fun for all ages.
3 The best storyteller I know is my uncle. <u>He</u> lived in India for several years.
4 We love listening to our English teacher. <u>Her</u> stories are fascinating.
5 At our school we have a great library. We like to relax and read <u>there</u>.

→ workbook page 46

Defining and non-defining relative clauses

3 Complete these sentences from the article on page 49. Then read the rule.

1 Remember, your novel, which will be fun to write, doesn't need to be 600 pages long.
2 You don't need to use long complex sentences or words that will leave your readers confused.

> **RULE:**
> We use a defining relative clause to identify an object, a person, a place or a possession. Without this information, it's hard to know who or what we're talking about.
> *We don't often see the people.* (Which people?)
> *We don't often see the people* ***who live next door.***
> We use a non-defining relative clause to add extra information. We don't need this information to understand the sentence. We put commas around it.
> *Roald Dahl was a famous writer.*
> *Roald Dahl,* ***who was British,*** *was a famous writer.*
> (Extra information: he was British.)

4 Complete these defining relative clauses with *who, where, whose* or *that*.

1 The house where I grew up is next to a school.
2 A book which has lots of short chapters is perfect for the bus ride to school.
3 A person who knows a lot of jokes is usually a good public speaker.
4 We went to hear a lecture by a writer whose books are always on the bestseller list.
5 The author who wrote the famous teen novel *The Outsiders* was only 16.

> **Look**
> We can only use *that* in defining relative clauses. In non-defining clauses we must use *which*.
> We can use *that* for people as well as things.

5 Tick (✓) the sentences which contain non-defining relative clauses and add commas.

1 My brother is someone who just doesn't like listening to jokes. ☐
2 Fairy tales which were written for children are now being adapted for the cinema. ☑
3 The Brothers Grimm whose stories have fascinated millions of children lived in the 19th century. ☑
4 It's difficult to read in places where people are talking on mobile phones. ☐

→ workbook page 46

VOCABULARY
Elements of a story

6 **Match the words with their definitions.**

character | dialogue | ending | hero
opening | plot | setting | villain

1 the story of a film, play, etc.
2 a person in a story
3 the last part of a story
4 the main (usually good) character in a story
5 a character who harms other people
6 the words that the characters say to each other
7 the beginning of a story
8 the time and place in which the action happens

7 **Think about these things for two minutes. Make notes.**

- a film or book with a great plot
- the setting of the last film you saw or story you read
- a film or book with a great opening
- a good film or book with a disappointing ending
- a film or book with a memorable villain

→ workbook page 48

8 SPEAKING **Work in pairs or small groups. Share your ideas.**

I really enjoyed the latest Spider-Man film – the plot was brilliant!

I don't think the ending of the book is very good.

All the characters in the story are fascinating, but the villain is the best!

LISTENING

9 **Find out how much your class knows about Roald Dahl. Then read the fact file.**

Roald Dahl FACT FILE

- Dahl was born in 1916 in Cardiff, Wales.
- His parents were immigrants from Norway.
- He was a fighter pilot during the Second World War.
- His first children's book was *The Gremlins*, which was published in 1942.
- His most famous book, *Charlie and the Chocolate Factory*, has sold over 13 million copies.
- Many of his books have been made into successful Hollywood movies, including *Charlie and the Chocolate Factory*, *Fantastic Mr Fox* and *The BFG*.

10 5.02 **Listen to two teenagers talking about a short story by Roald Dahl called *The Hitchhiker*. In the story, he uses an invented word: 'fingersmith'. What does a fingersmith do?**

11 5.02 **Listen again and answer the questions.**

1 Why is Annie surprised that Lucy is reading Roald Dahl?
2 What was *Tales of the Unexpected*?
3 What was Roald Dahl's connection to it?
4 Who are the two main characters in *The Hitchhiker*?
5 Why does the policeman stop them?
6 What does the policeman write down in his book?
7 What does the hitchhiker do to show how good he is with his fingers?
8 Why isn't the hitchhiker worried about the policeman?

12 SPEAKING **Compare your answers in pairs.**

READING

1 **Look at the titles. Have you seen any of the film versions of the books? What did you think of them?**

2 **Read the magazine article and title quickly. Decide which paragraph is *for* and which is *against* the argument.**

3 5.03 **Read and listen to the article. Answer the questions.**

1 What does Ellie like doing when she's reading a book?
2 Why wasn't she disappointed by the film of *The Lord of the Rings*?
3 Why didn't she like the film version of *The Maze Runner*?
4 Why does Ben prefer films to books?
5 What did he think of *The Hunger Games* books?
6 Why does he try and watch films of the books he has to read for school?

4 SPEAKING **Work in pairs. Discuss.**

1 Which do you prefer to do first: read the original book or watch the film version of it?
2 Think of a film that you think was much better or worse than the book. Say why.

LORD OF THE FLIES
THE MAZE RUNNER
THE HUNGER GAMES
The Lord of the Rings
The Jungle Book

WRITING
A short paragraph expressing an opinion

5 **Write a paragraph giving your ideas on the statement: 'Books are always better than their films.'**

1 Say what your opinion is and why.
2 Give examples from books you've read and films you've seen.

THERE ARE ALWAYS TWO SIDES TO AN ARGUMENT

BOOKS ARE ALWAYS BETTER THAN THEIR FILMS.

When you read a book, you can imagine it all in your head: what the characters look like, where the action takes place – that sort of thing. Then when you see the film, you can compare your ideas with those of the director, which is always interesting. If you see the film first, you don't get to use your own imagination because you just see things the way they were in the film. It's a shame and I don't really see the point in doing it. For example, I read *The Lord of the Rings* and had all these wonderful images in my head. When I saw the films, which were directed by the great Peter Jackson, some of it was quite different from how I had imagined it, but it didn't matter. His visions were so brilliant and I wasn't disappointed. It doesn't always work like that, though. Sometimes the film version can be a real disappointment. I saw *The Maze Runner* a few weeks ago. I loved that book, but the film just wasn't right for me. In my opinion, the characters were all wrong and they'd changed some of my favourite bits. I didn't bother to see the other films in the series. I didn't want to spoil my own personal memories of the books.

Ellie

I hardly ever read books, so I nearly always see the film first. I think it's probably because I'm a bit lazy. It takes me weeks to finish a book whereas I can watch the film in 90 minutes, which leaves me time to do other things. But sometimes I enjoy a film so much that it makes me want to go and read the book. I love fantasy and science fiction stories and so I did that with *The Hunger Games* series. The films were amazing, so I went out and bought the books. It took me a bit of time to get through them, but they were worth the time and effort. I really enjoyed them, even though I knew what was going to happen. It was also quite interesting seeing where the film and book were a bit different. When our teacher asks us to read books for school, I always see if I can get a film of the book first. That helps me get into the books, which are often quite difficult. If I already know what the story is about, it helps me understand better when I'm reading. I did this with *Lord of the Flies* and *The Jungle Book*. Seeing the films first really helped me enjoy the books more.

Ben

GRAMMAR
Relative clauses with *which*

6 Complete these sentences from the article on page 52. What does *which* refer to in each of the sentences? Complete the rule.

1 I can watch the film in 90 minutes, __which__ leaves me time to do other things.

2 You can compare your ideas with those of the director, __which__ is always interesting.

> **RULE:** The pronoun [3] __which__ normally refers to a noun, but it can sometimes refer to the whole of the previous clause. We cannot use [4] __which__ or *that* in the same way.
> *She was late, which made her nervous.*

7 Join the pairs of sentences using *which*.

0 I often play the drums on Sunday mornings. This annoys the neighbours.
I often play *the drums on Sunday mornings, which annoys* the neighbours.

1 She's lost all her money. This means she'll be in trouble.
She's lost __all her money, which means she will be__ in trouble.

2 Nobody in class learned the new words. It was frustrating for our teacher.
Nobody in class __learned the new words, which was frustrating__ for our teacher.

3 Fairy tales have been turned into successful teen films. This has surprised many people.
Fairy tales __have been turned into successful teen films, which has surprised__ many people.

4 It's quite amazing that the author manages to write several books per year.
She __manages to write several books per year, which__ quite amazing.

5 It's fascinating that most of his books have been made into films.
Most of his books __have been made into films, which is__ fascinating.

8 Complete the sentences so that they are true for you.

0 My favourite singer *is giving a concert in our town next month*, which is fantastic.

1 __I organized my friend's birthday__ last year, which made me feel really proud.

2 I heard on the news that __someone had died in a car accident__, which I was really upset about.

3 __I have four tests next week__, which really isn't easy.

9 SPEAKING Work in pairs. Share your sentences. How long can you keep each conversation going?

My favourite singer Dua Lipa is giving a concert in our town soon.

Wow! I like her songs, too. Do you know when ...?

→ workbook page 47

VOCABULARY
Types of story

10 5.04 Match the types of story with the book covers. Write numbers 1–7 in the boxes. Then listen and check.

1 crime novel
2 science fiction novel
3 historical novel
4 horror story
5 (auto)biography
6 romantic novel
7 fantasy novel

11 Which type of story is non-fiction?

12 SPEAKING Which types of story do you like reading most?

→ workbook page 48

SPEAKING

13 Work in pairs. If you had to choose one of the books in the previous exercise, which would it be and why?

I'd choose ... because the cover looks / the title sounds (exciting / funny / interesting / ...).

14 Prepare a one-minute talk about reading. Think about the following points and take notes.

- if you prefer articles, short stories, novels, etc.
- where and when you like reading

15 Take turns giving your talks in small groups.

TH!NK

Storytelling in the Caribbean

Culture

1 Look at the photos and answer the questions.

1. What can you see in the photos?
2. What do you think the person is doing?
3. Would you like to visit this place? Why or why not?

2 5.05 **Read and listen to the article. Find out who Paul Keens-Douglas and Tanti Merle are.**

Storytelling in the Caribbean

Storytelling plays a big part in the childhood of most people growing up on the Caribbean Islands. It is a tradition that was brought over from Africa by their ancestors many years ago and is a way of keeping their shared culture alive. The stories are a way of remembering the past and making sure it's not forgotten in the future.

And despite the modern distractions of television and video games, many Caribbean families still gather on the steps outside their homes, with the full moon in the sky and the wind blowing gently through the palm trees, to hear stories that they have already heard many times before.

The storyteller has an important position in Caribbean society. But it is not an art that is learned quickly. Good storytellers take years to perfect their performances. First, they must collect a catalogue of good stories, which are often short and simple and should work well for people of all ages. They must then practise these on family members to test out their material before moving on to larger crowds in local community centres. From there they may choose to become travelling storytellers and move from town to town looking for new audiences to share their tales with. And the very best storytellers make it onto the international stage and travel the world. More recently many storytellers have started using film to reach even more people.

With many Caribbean islands and people originating from many African countries, there are lots of types of stories to be told. One common feature though is the performance tradition known as 'crick crack'. Although this may differ a little in each country, the basic idea is that the audience participates in the storytelling. For example, in St Lucia, where stories are usually told in French, the storyteller (known as the 'conteur') announces that he or she wants to tell a story by shouting out 'Crick!' and the audience show they want to listen by responding 'Crack!' Throughout the performance, the storyteller continues to involve the audience by inviting them to answer questions and riddles and to make comments. In this way, the storyteller and the audience become an almost equally important part of the whole experience.

But as well as the many traditional tales and myths there are to be told, storytellers also create their own characters, and the most successful of these have become part of cultural life. One of the most famous storytellers in the West Indies is Paul Keens-Douglas, who was born in Trinidad but grew up in Grenada. Probably his most popular character, Tanti Merle, is known throughout the region and appears in many of his stories. Tanti Merle is a woman who is not afraid to say what she thinks and Keens-Douglas uses her as a lovable comic figure to make comments on everyday life in the Caribbean.

3 Read the article again. Mark the sentences T (true) or F (false).

1. Children in the Caribbean don't use modern technology. ☐
2. Storytellers have to learn long detailed stories. ☐
3. Audiences play an important part in the storytelling. ☐
4. You should shout 'crack' if you want to hear a story. ☐
5. Storytellers only tell traditional stories. ☐

4 SPEAKING **Work in pairs. Discuss these questions.**

1. How does the Caribbean storytelling tradition compare with storytelling in your country?
2. What stories are there about places near where you live?

5 VOCABULARY There are eight highlighted words or phrases in the text. Match the words with these meanings. Write the words.

1 short word puzzles
2 lots of people together
3 is present
4 the art, stories and history of a place
5 takes part in something
6 a collection of something
7 normal
8 things that take your attention from what you are doing

SPEAKING

6 Look at the pictures. Put them in order and use them to tell a story.

A

B

C

7 5.08 Listen and compare your story to the one you hear.

PRONUNCIATION
The schwa /ə/ in word endings Go to page 120.

FUNCTIONS
Telling a story

8 5.08 Annie uses these expressions to bring her story to life. Match them with the correct places in the conversation. Then listen again and check.

☐ you'll never believe what
☐ The strangest thing happened to me the other day.
☐ Well, let me finish …
☐ That was the annoying thing.
☐ What are the chances?

Annie 1 ____________
Mac What?
Annie I woke up with this song in my head and I couldn't stop singing it all day long. It was really annoying.
Mac What was it?
Annie 2 ____________ It was a song I knew, but I couldn't remember what it was. I even sang it to a few of my friends, but they didn't know what it was either.
Mac So what was so strange about that?
Annie 3 ____________ I got home from school (with the song still in my head) and I went upstairs to do my homework. I decided to put on the radio to try and forget the song, and 4 ____________ they were playing!
Mac Go on.
Annie They were playing the song that I'd been singing all day!
Mac So you'd just been singing a pop song that you'd forgotten the name of.
Annie Yes, but the strange thing is that it wasn't a pop song from now. It was some obscure song from the 1980s that you never hear any more. It was a song that my dad used to play when I was really small. I hadn't heard it for years. And they were playing it on the radio! 5 ____________
Mac Yes, that is pretty weird.

9 Think of a strange story that happened to you or to someone else.

- Write down the main events in note form.
- Think how you can use some of the expressions.
- In groups, tell your stories.

6 THAT'S IMPOSSIBLE

OBJECTIVES

FUNCTIONS:
talking about sequence; explaining how things are done

GRAMMAR:
present and past passive (review); *have something done*; future and present perfect passive (review)

VOCABULARY:
extreme adjectives and modifiers; *make* and *do*

Get THINKING

Watch the video and think: what is your favourite magic trick?

READING

1 SPEAKING **Work in pairs. Discuss these questions.**

1 What magicians can you name?
2 What magic tricks have you seen?
3 Can you do any tricks yourself? What are they?

2 **Read the article about David Copperfield quickly. Which three of his tricks does it mention?**

3 6.01 **Read and listen to the article again and match the sentences (a–g) with the spaces (1–6). There's one extra sentence which doesn't belong in the text. Check your answers.**

a It was very dark and he fell. ☐
b The audience is absolutely amazed. ☐
c Where had he gone? ☐
d Time and time again, people have wondered: ☐
e There was nothing there. ☐
f He walked in one side and out the other. ☐
g People who catch one are invited to come up onto the stage. ☐

Train to THINK

Understanding what's relevant

To write a good text, a writer must make sure that each sentence is linked to what comes before it. Understanding how this is done will help you to do tasks like Exercise 3.

4 **Choose the sentence which *doesn't* have any relevance to the first.**

David Copperfield made the Statue of Liberty disappear.
A He was watched by millions on TV.
B He performed in front of a live audience.
C People from all over the world visit the statue every year.
D He used a large sheet to hide the statue.

5 SPEAKING **Work in pairs. Use this sentence to make a similar task for your partner.**

Gavin Cox was injured in one of David Copperfield's magic tricks.
A ____________ C ____________
B ____________ D ____________

HOW ON EARTH DOES HE DO IT?

Perhaps the world's most famous magician, David Copperfield has entertained his audiences for years with his fantastic magic tricks and thrilling illusions. [1]_____ 'How did he do that?'

The Great Wall

In a 1986 TV special, Copperfield appeared to walk *through* the Great Wall of China. [2]_____ First, he stepped into a box and the audience could see his silhouette on the white screens around the box. Then, he appeared to enter the wall. Minutes later his silhouette could be seen pushing out through the wall into a similar box on the other side. The white screens were lifted and there stood the magician, on the other side of the wall.

The Statue of Liberty

A live TV event was staged in April 1983. A huge audience sat on Liberty Island in New York Harbour, facing the Statue of Liberty. There was a column on each side of the stage and the statue was visible between the two columns. A white screen was raised and the statue was hidden from view. Minutes later, the screen was lowered, and to the amazement of the audience, the statue had disappeared. [3]_____ Then, as the stunned audience watched, the screen was raised again. But this time, when it was lowered, the Statue of Liberty was there again.

Lucky 13

Imagine the scene at one of David Copperfield's shows. From the stage, 13 soft balls are thrown into the audience. [4]_____ These 13 volunteers enter a cage, which is raised above the stage. The people inside are given torches to shine at the audience, and then a cover is lowered over them. When the magician lifts the cover, the cage is empty – but then, moments later, the 13 people reappear at the back of the theatre, still holding the torches they were given. [5]_____ This is David Copperfield's famous Lucky 13 trick, which he performed for nearly 20 years. How did he do it?

The secret revealed

Normally magicians guard their secrets, but this time we know the answer. In 2013, 55-year-old chef Gavin Cox was at one of Copperfield's shows in Las Vegas. He was called up to the stage by the magician to take part in the Lucky 13 illusion. As soon as the cage was covered, he and the other 12 volunteers were pushed quickly into a secret passage and outside the theatre. In the confusion, Mr Cox was injured. "They were shouting 'Hurry! Run, run, run'," he said. He didn't know where he was going. [6]_____ After the accident, there was a court case and Copperfield had to reveal the trick and the technique of his famous 'disappearing audience' illusion.

SPEAKING

6 Work in pairs. Discuss these questions.

1 What other magic tricks can you think of?
2 How do you think the Great Wall and the Statue of Liberty tricks were done?

PRONUNCIATION
The /ʒ/ phoneme Go to page 120.

GRAMMAR

Present and past passive (review)

1 Complete these sentences from the article on page 57. Use the correct form of *be*. Then complete the rule with *by*, *be* and *past participle*.

1 Gavin Cox ______ called up to the stage by the magician.
2 Thirteen soft balls ______ thrown into the audience.
3 The white screens ______ lifted.
4 The cage ______ raised above the stage.

RULE: We form the passive with a form of the verb [5] ______ and the [6] ______ .
We use the preposition [7] ______ to say who or what does the action, but only if this is important.

2 Complete the instructions with the correct active or passive forms of the verbs.

cut | get | hide | hold | pull | push | ~~use~~

0 A long box *is used* for this trick.
1 One woman ______________ at one end of the box.
2 A second woman ______________ into the box.
3 She puts her head out of one end and ______________ her legs to her chest with her arms. At the same time, the first woman ______________ her legs out of the other end.
4 The box ______________ in half by the magician.
5 The ends of the box ______________ apart to show that it has been cut in two.

→ workbook page 54

VOCABULARY

Extreme adjectives and modifiers

3 Look at these phrases from the article on page 57. What do the adjectives in bold mean?

1 As the **stunned** audience watched, the screen was raised again.
2 A **huge** audience sat on Liberty Island.
3 David Copperfield has entertained his audiences for years with his **fantastic** magic tricks and **thrilling** illusions.

4 Match the gradable adjectives (1–8) with the extreme adjectives (a–h).

1 good	a hilarious
2 funny	b fascinating
3 happy	c huge / enormous
4 big	d freezing
5 small	e great / fantastic / wonderful / brilliant / amazing
6 bad	f delighted
7 cold	g tiny / minute
8 interesting	h terrible

Look

We use:
- *very* with gradable adjectives.
- *absolutely* with extreme adjectives.
- *really* with gradable and extreme adjectives.

5 Look at these examples of adjectives with the modifiers *very*, *really* and *absolutely*. Which combinations are correct and which are incorrect? Mark them ✓ or ✗.

1 really good ☐
2 really amazing ☐
3 very funny ☐
4 very hilarious ☐
5 absolutely small ☐
6 absolutely tiny ☐

6 Complete the text with adjectives from Exercise 4. Sometimes more than one answer is possible, but don't use each adjective more than once.

Last night, we went to a magic show. It was very good – in fact, it was absolutely [1] ______ . The magician was really [2] ______ – we couldn't stop laughing. In one trick, he had two hats: a really small one and an [3] ______ one. But from the big hat he pulled out an absolutely [4] ______ rabbit and from the small hat he pulled out a huge one. It was great fun and I left feeling really [5] ______ .

→ workbook page 56

LISTENING

7 6.04 **Listen to two people talking about a haircut. What is unusual about James' haircut?**

8 6.04 **Listen again. Tick (✓) the reasons why Mia is so upset about James's haircut.**

1 It was expensive. ☐
2 He'll spoil his sister's wedding photos. ☐
3 It looks silly. ☐
4 He missed his date with her. ☐
5 His parents will be angry. ☐
6 It was done badly. ☐

9 **Replace the underlined words or phrases with the words below from the dialogue.**

centre of attention | furious | a work of art
must be joking | a disaster

1 It's <u>a brilliant creation</u>.
2 It's <u>extremely bad</u>.
3 She should be the <u>person everyone is looking at</u>.
4 You <u>can't be serious</u>.
5 They will be <u>very angry</u>.

GRAMMAR

have something done

10 **Underline the subject in each sentence. Do we know who is performing the action? Then complete the rule with *us* and *someone*.**

1 I've had my hair cut.
2 I can have the lizard shaved off.
3 I'm going to have my arms tattooed.

RULE: We often use the structure ***have*** + object + past participle when we arrange for [4]______ to do something for [5]______ . In less formal contexts, *get* often replaces *have*.

11 **Complete the sentences. Use *have* + object + past participle.**

Lord Uppity doesn't do anything himself.
1 He never cooks. He ______ his meals ______ by chefs.
2 He and his wife never do any housework. They ______ it ______ by cleaners.
3 He never goes into shops. He ______ everything ______ by his assistant.
4 Neither he nor his wife drives. They ______ their car ______ by an ex-racing driver.
5 They never organise parties. They ______ them ______ by party organisers.
6 They don't look after their children. They ______ them ______ by a nanny.
Life is boring. There's simply nothing to do!

12 **Use the words to write questions.**

car | clean | ~~cut~~ | do | ~~hair~~ | make
repair | tattoo | teeth | wedding cake

0 *Where can you have your hair cut*?
At the To Dye For salon.
1 ______________________? At Derek's Bakery.
2 ______________________? At Bridge Street Mechanic's.
3 ______________________? At Body Art.
4 ______________________? At the Northgate Dental Surgery.

→ workbook page 54

SPEAKING

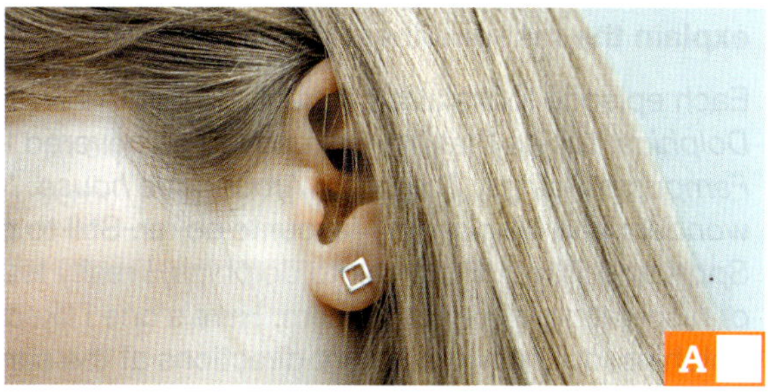

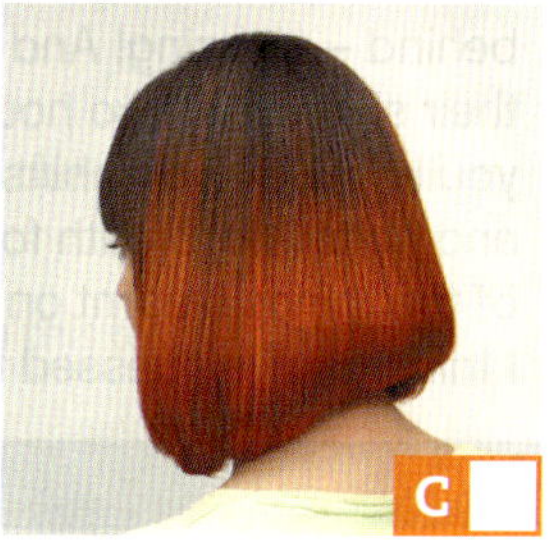

13 **Match the photos with 1–3.**

1 'My parents won't let me have my hair dyed.'
2 'Dad was right. What a bad idea it was to get a tattoo!'
3 'I'm not allowed to get my ears pierced.'

14 **Work in pairs. Think of possible reasons for these teenagers' parents' attitudes.**

15 **How do you feel about these issues? Tell your partner.**

Fiction

1 What is a 'mind map'? What do people use them for?

2 6.06 Read and listen to the extract. What two things surprise Lucho very much?

THE MIND MAP

BY DAVID MORRISON

Lucho and Eva are classmates at a school in Salvador. Their teacher tells them to make a mind map together. Lucho starts one at home, around the word *guaca*, which are special gold objects made by South American tribes. At home Lucho has a gold pendant that his grandmother gave him. Here, Lucho and Eva go to a computer to find more information for the mind map Lucho started.

Eva typed 'Kogi' and pressed Enter. […] Soon [she] had found the web page she was looking for.

'OK.' Eva started reading. 'The Sierra Nevada mountains are home to the Kogi tribe. The ancestors of the Kogi were the brave Tairona …,' she continued. 'Like their ancestors, the Kogi still make things from gold.'

'Should I write this down?' asked Lucho.

'Of course, or we will forget it,' Eva answered.

Lucho put his notebook on the table next to the computer and looked at the screen, where there was a photograph of a Kogi chief. The chief was wearing a jaguar skin and he had jaguar teeth on a piece of gold string round his neck. He seemed to be looking straight at Lucho from the screen. […]

'What are you waiting for, Lucho? Write these things on your mind map!' Eva said.

[Lucho] opened his notebook and turned to the page where he had drawn his mind map, but when he saw what had happened, he almost fell off his chair.

'Eva, something's wrong!' Lucho shouted.

'Shh!' said Eva. 'We're in the library!'

'The mind map has changed, Eva. Look!'

He showed her the mind map. There were words now in the four circles he had drawn with the pendant. The words were, 'Nebtashi', 'Hotel Continental', 'Esmeralda' and 'Ichua'.

'I don't even write like that, Eva!'

'Lucho,' said Eva, 'this is not the time for silly jokes. We don't have much time before the next class.'

'Eva, I promise. All I did last night was to draw the circles and the lines and write "guaca" in the centre circle. Something amazing has happened!'

Eva stood up.

'I'm sorry, Lucho.' Her voice was very serious now. 'I don't think you're a bad person, but you are a little strange. I will do the mind map alone. You can tell your story to Mr Parra on Monday.'

Eva walked out of the library. Lucho didn't know what to think. How had the words appeared on the mind map? Something strange, something very strange, was happening.

Quickly, he typed 'Ichua' into the computer, but couldn't find any information. He now knew that 'Nebtashi' meant 'jaguar', and 'Esmeralda' was his grandmother's name. He looked for information about the 'Hotel Continental', but could only find pages about hotels in places he had never heard of.

'I must show Eva that I'm not lying!' he said to himself as he put his notebook and pen into his bag and stood up. Suddenly he sat down again. Big red letters had started to appear on the computer screen and slowly the letters became words, three words:

'TAKE IT BACK.'

Lucho could not believe his eyes.

3 Read the extract again. Answer the questions.

1 What do the Kogi people still do now that they did in the past?
2 Why does Lucho open his notebook?
3 Why does Lucho almost fall off his chair?
4 Why does Eva leave the library?
5 What does Lucho look for after Eva leaves?
6 What does Lucho want to prove to Eva?

4 SPEAKING Work in pairs and answer the questions.

1 What do you think 'it' could be in the message on Lucho's screen?
2 What might the words in the mind map mean?
3 Why has he been told to 'take it back'?

FUNCTIONS
Talking about sequence

5 SPEAKING Work in pairs. In what order do these things happen when an aeroplane takes off? Number the boxes. Discuss your ideas.

First, I think ... *After that, ...* *Next, ...* *Finally, ...*

The engine is powered up.

The brakes are taken off.

The wheels are pulled up.

The plane is turned around in the air.

The nose is lifted into the air.

The plane is lined up on the runway.

WRITING
Explaining how things are done

1 INPUT Read the explanation and check your answers to the last exercise.

HOW DO PLANES TAKE OFF?

To get an aeroplane into the air, you need the correct airspeed. Airspeed is not the speed of the plane, but how fast the air is moving over it. If the plane is facing a strong wind, the airspeed is already quite high. That's why planes are usually lined up to take off facing into the wind.

The engines are turned up to a certain power. Then the brakes are taken off and the plane speeds down the runway. As it does this, air passes over the wings. The wings are curved on the top, so the air has further to travel over the wings than under the wings, and has to travel faster. This creates a force that pushes upwards. When that force is big enough, the nose of the plane is pushed into the air and when the correct airspeed is reached, the whole plane takes off.

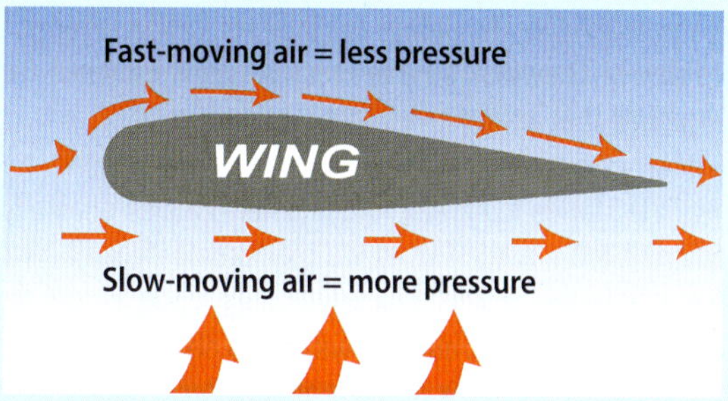

When the plane is high enough in the air, the wheels are pulled up and the plane is turned around, leaving space for the next one to take off.

2 ANALYSE Read the explanation again. Then make two lists for ...

- the procedure (what happens and in what order).
- the theories (explanations of why things happen).

3 PRODUCE Choose an activity from the list or your own idea. Write an explanation of how to do it (150 words).

- how to play the guitar
- how to play your favourite computer game
- how to do a headstand

Think about:

- the procedure and the sequence.
- whether you need to explain any theories.
- how to explain any difficult vocabulary.

TOWARDS B2 First for Schools

READING AND USE OF ENGLISH
Multiple choice

→ workbook page 61

1 You are going to read a text about urban legends. For questions 1–4, choose the answer (A, B, C or D) which you think fits best according to the text.

People have been telling stories for as long as they have been walking the Earth. And from cave paintings to Shakespeare's Globe Theatre to Hollywood blockbusters, the methods of telling them have got more and more sophisticated.

In the 1960s, a new storytelling art form emerged – the urban legend. Even if you've never heard the term, you've certainly heard an urban legend. What about the story of the unwanted pet alligators that were flushed down the toilet and are now living in the sewers of New York City? Or the man who woke up in a bathtub full of ice and saw a note informing him that one of his kidneys had been taken out?

One of the key features of the urban legend is its lack of an author. The stories appear mysteriously and are then passed on by word of mouth. And although we know these mini-tales of horror, humour and embarrassment are almost certainly not true, part of us wants to believe them.

Then the internet, which is packed with fiction (everything from jokes to the latest releases from top-selling authors), helped create and spread urban legends. Before the internet, urban legends went around quite slowly. They took time to reach a larger audience. The internet changed all that almost overnight.

The internet is the perfect vehicle for the urban legend, for it not only allows the stories to spread much faster but also allows for greater anonymity, too – a lot of what we read online doesn't have an author's name attached to it. This anonymity adds to the overall mystery.

Of course, the internet also allows you to check the truth of a story more easily. Over time, a number of sites have appeared which collect stories, investigate their origins and report the results. Often there isn't any truth to the story at all. But sometimes the urban legend grew from something that did actually happen. Thanks to the internet, learning about the origins of an urban legend can be as interesting and entertaining as the story itself.

1 What do we learn about stories from the first paragraph?
- A They've never been as popular as they are now.
- B They have their origins in the days of Shakespeare.
- C They were much longer in the past.
- D Ways of telling them have changed over time.

2 What does the author suggest about urban legends?
- A Everyone knows the term 'urban legend'.
- B Everyone knows an example of one.
- C They appeared at the same time as the internet.
- D They're always about horrific events.

3 What does the author mean when he says 'the internet … is packed with fiction'?
- A You can find every story written online.
- B You can get most fiction for free online.
- C There are lots of stories on the internet.
- D There are too many stories on the internet.

4 What does the author suggest about urban legends in the last paragraph?
- A They're generally mystery stories.
- B They're usually short.
- C Nowadays it's easier to discover if they're true or not.
- D Some include the author's name.

VOCABULARY

1 Complete the sentences with the words in the list. There are four extra words.

character | delighted | ending | enormous | fascinating | freezing
hero | hilarious | opening | plot | setting | terrible | tiny | villain

1 The ________________ of the film is an amazing doctor who can travel through time and save people.
2 The show that we saw in the theatre last night was ________________ . I couldn't stop laughing.
3 I've just read the last page of the book, and I don't like the ________________ .
4 I couldn't read all the words very well because the letters were ________________ .
5 He dived into the ________________ water.
6 There is one ________________ in the film who is really funny. He makes everybody laugh.
7 I haven't done my homework. I had a ________________ headache last night.
8 I can't put this book down – it's ________________ . I'm learning so much!
9 I'm ________________ that you can come and see the show. The other actors will be happy, too.
10 The ________________ of the story is an evil vampire.

/10

GRAMMAR

2 Complete the sentences with the words/phrases in the list. There are two extra words/phrases.

are used | have it removed | have been taken | whose | where | who | that | are pulled

1 It's a story ________________ has been passed down from generation to generation.
2 Hundreds of photos of the magician ________________ .
3 She's an actor ________________ has a great talent for storytelling.
4 Jack had a tattoo done a few years ago, and now he wants to ________________ .
5 Two rabbits ________________ out of a hat in this trick.
6 He still lives in the city ________________ he was born.

3 Find and correct the mistake in each sentence.

1 The decision will be done by the judges tonight.
2 I didn't make very well in the test.
3 The marathon will have shown live on TV.
4 I won a medal for swimming last term, what made me feel proud.
5 I'm not allowed have my hair dyed.
6 Mrs Jones, who son I went to school with, is my piano teacher.

/12

FUNCTIONAL LANGUAGE

4 Choose the correct words.

1 A You'll never *know* / *believe* what happened just now.
B *What* / *Really*?
A I guessed all the answers in the TV quiz show correctly. What are the *chances* / *opportunities* of that?
2 A What's that song you keep singing?
B That's the *annoying* / *angry* thing! I can't remember what it's called or who sings it.
3 A How does this machine work, then?
B First, the engine *is* / *was* turned on. After *it* / *that*, the handbrake is released.
4 A My dyed hair is a work of art!
B A work of art? You must be *laughing* / *joking*.

/8

MY SCORE /30

22–30 | 10–21 | 0–9

7 BREAKING AWAY

OBJECTIVES

FUNCTIONS: talking about permission; talking about habits; invitations

GRAMMAR: *make / let* and *be allowed to*; *be / get used to*

VOCABULARY: phrasal verbs (1); personality; phrases with *all*

Get THINKING

Watch the video and think: who is the oldest person you know?

READING

1 **Look at the photos. What can you see? Use these words to help you.**

ironing | rugby | surfing

2 **Answer the questions.**

1 Do any of the photos make you laugh? If so, why?
2 Do you think any of the photos are strange? If so, why?
3 Do you think the photos have anything in common?

3 **Read the text that your teacher tells you to read (A or B). Answer the questions.**

1 Who is the text about?
2 In what way did the person do something different?
3 Who tried to stop the person from doing what they wanted to do?
4 Who (if anyone) helped the person?
5 What long-term effect did the person's actions have?

4 SPEAKING **Work in pairs. Using your answers to Exercise 3, tell your partner about your person.**

5 7.01 **Now read and listen to both texts. Answer the questions.**

1 How did Kathrine Switzer usually write her name?
2 What happened to Switzer after the race?
3 How much slower was Switzer fifty years later?
4 Why did Hogan not go to medical school?
5 Why did Hogan choose to go to MUW?
6 Why did MUW have to accept Hogan as a student?

Train to THINK

Thinking outside the box

In problem-solving, it can be useful to think really imaginatively, trying to avoid obvious or standard ideas. We call this 'thinking outside the box'. Sometimes thinking of very different possible answers to a problem helps us find the best solution.

It isn't a question of intelligence, just of thinking freely and creatively. The more you try it, the easier it is.

6 **Complete the table with as many ideas as you can think of.**

Questions about the texts	My 'outside the box ideas'
1 Why did Semple want to stop Switzer?	*He wanted to get his photo in the newspapers.*
2 Why were a lot of women at MUW against letting Hogan in?	

7 **How many 'outside the box' answers can you think of for these questions?**

1 What weighs more than it did half a year ago?
2 What are things money can't buy?
3 What can you do at school but not at home?

CHANGING THE RULES

A CHANGING THE MARATHON

In 1967, runner 261 was just one of hundreds of competitors in the Boston Marathon – KV Switzer. But something was different. The race started and soon spectators and photographers realised that KV Switzer was … a woman.

Back then, there was no rule that women couldn't run official long-distance races – they simply didn't, and many thought they wouldn't want to. When Kathrine Switzer registered for the marathon, she wrote her initials as she always did, so no one found out she was a woman. When she showed up for the race, none of the race officials noticed, so when the starter fired the gun, she set off.

But after about six kilometres, an official called Jock Semple wanted to make her stop. He ran out, grabbed her and tried to pull her off the road. Switzer's friend Tom Miller pushed Semple away, and Switzer carried on running. She finished the race in 4 hours 20 minutes.

After the race, Switzer was banned from entering athletics events because she had run with men. However, newspaper reports of her run made many people question their ideas about women and running. In 1972, public opinion forced the organisers of the Boston Marathon to let women compete. One of them was Switzer. Later, she went on to play an important role as a campaigner, which led to the first ever women's Olympic marathon in the 1984 Games.

In 2017, Switzer ran the Boston Marathon again, aged 70. She finished in 4 hours 44 minutes. And the organisers retired number 261 – no one will use that number again.

B MALE STUDENT IN AN ALL-WOMEN COLLEGE

Joe Hogan took up nursing as a young man. He didn't have many qualifications, but he started working at a community hospital in Mississippi, US. In 1981, he decided that he wanted to get higher qualifications. He didn't have enough money to go to medical school, so he applied for a course in nursing. One option he had was to enrol at the University of Mississippi, but that was almost 200 km away from his home. He didn't want to move, or to travel that far every day – so he applied to the Mississippi University for Women (MUW).

MUW leaders turned him down – as a college for women only, it did not allow men to study there. But Joe didn't give up. He went to court, but he lost the first time. He went to court again and in 1982, after a year of arguments, a panel of nine judges decided that MUW had to accept Joe as a student. The president of MUW (a man) was furious, and many of the students (women) thought the decision was wrong and that the college should not let Hogan enrol. But the college, in the end, had no choice – and Hogan joined. MUW ended up accepting men on all its courses (not just nursing) and now a small number of men study there. The college has not changed its name, however.

SPEAKING

8 Work in pairs. Discuss these questions.

1. If you could meet either Switzer or Hogan, which one would you choose? What questions would you ask her or him?
2. Do you know any stories about someone who tried to change a situation they thought was wrong? Tell your partner.

READING

1 **Look at the photos and the title. What do you think the article is about?**

A two men who built a prison
B a man whose father went to prison and became president
C a friendship between a prisoner and a prison warden
D a friendship between two prisoners

2 **Read the article quickly. Check your answer to Exercise 1.**

3 **7.03 Read the article again. At each point 1–6, choose the best answer. Then listen to check your answers.**

4 **Answer the questions.**

1 Where did Brand spend his childhood?
2 What kind of prisoners was Brand told he was going to work with?
3 What did Brand and Mandela have in common?
4 Why did Mandela and Brand have to keep their friendship secret?
5 What did Mandela do for Brand when he became president?

MY PRISONER, MY FRIEND,
MY PRESIDENT AND MY FATHER

In 1978, Christo Brand joined the prison service. He was an 18-year-old white South African boy who had grown up on a farm. Now he was being sent to work as a warden in the famous prison on Robben Island. There, he was told, he was going to work with the biggest criminals in South African history, including political prisoners. Brand didn't know very much about [1]*politics / prisoners* – he just knew that he was going to work with some dangerous people.

And then he met prisoner 46664, a quiet 60-year-old black man who started to talk to Brand and ask him questions – questions about his family, his education, his plans for the [2]*future / prison*. Prisoner 46664 was Nelson Mandela, who would one day become the first black president of South Africa.

'There was no [3]*language / colour* barrier between us,' said Brand, who later worked as a guide showing tourists around Robben Island. 'Like me, Mandela came from a farm. We understood that we shared the same sky and the same air.' The two men got on well and became quite close, although this wasn't allowed by the prison authorities. They had to keep their friendship secret and their conversations had to be [4]*short / fascinating*. Brand found that Mandela was a warm and thoughtful person, even a little shy sometimes.

Mandela was also a generous man and he never forgot his friend. When he became president, he got Brand a job. One day, at a meeting of important politicians, Brand was in the room and was putting documents on the table. When Mandela came in, he saw Brand, went to him and hugged him. Mandela looked at [5]*Brand / all the people in the room* and said, 'This person was my warden. This person was my [6]*friend / teacher*.' Brand says that he felt very proud at that moment.

Nelson Mandela died in December 2013, aged 95. Like so many people around the world, Brand was very sad when he heard the news. He said at the time, 'Mandela was my prisoner, my friend, my president and my father.'

VOCABULARY
Personality

5 Read the sentences about the listening on page 69 and the article on page 70. Choose the correct words.

1 Everyone in India was *shy and rude* / *warm and kind* even when we didn't understand each other well.
2 Some people can be *cold and unfriendly* / *lively and polite* but everyone I met was really nice.
3 The writer describes Mandela as a *lively and selfish* / *generous and thoughtful* man.

6 Which adjectives in Exercise 5 are positive, negative and neutral? Mark them +, – or 0. Use a dictionary to check the meaning of any of the words that you are unsure of.

7 Which adjectives describe each person? You can choose more than one for each person.

1 *No, it's mine. You can't use it.*

2 *I don't want to go to the party, thanks. I'm not comfortable with strangers.*

3 *Jack's had some bad news. Let's go and talk to him. Perhaps he needs a friend.*

4 *Don't worry. There's a problem, but everything's going to be all right, OK?*

5 *Go away! I'm working. I don't want to talk to you now.*

8 Complete each response with an adjective. There may be more than one possible answer.

1 A Hey, you! Get out of my way!
B What a ______ boy!
2 A The children aren't tired at all.
B Yes, they're very ______ tonight.
3 A Let's all go and have a hamburger. I'll pay.
B Wow! That's very ______ of you.
4 A He always says 'please' and 'thank you'.
B Yes, he's very ______ .
5 A She never laughs or cries or anything.
B I know. She's a bit ______ sometimes.
6 A Mandy always thinks about other people.
B Yes, she's a really ______ person.

9 Write four sentences about people you know. (You don't need to use their names!) Use adjectives from Exercise 5 and give reasons.

I know someone who I think is rude because he/she never says hello at the bus stop.

10 SPEAKING **Compare your sentences with the class.**

→ workbook page 66

TH!NK values
Stereotypes

11 SPEAKING **Work in small groups. Discuss these questions.**

1 Think about your own country, or a region of your country. Do people from other places have fixed ideas about the people who live there?

Some people think the British are very polite but not very friendly.

2 Why do you think people have these ideas?
3 Do you think there is any truth in the stereotypes of your country or region?

12 Some stereotypes are about nationalities. What other groups of people are there stereotypes about? Write a list. Then compare your ideas.

People who live in small towns …

13 SPEAKING **In your groups, discuss stereotypes that you think people have about teenagers.**

WRITING
An article about stereotypes

14 Write an article (80–120 words) for a school magazine about a national stereotype. Think about:

- a culture that some people in your country see as a stereotype.
  In Britain, a lot of people think that Americans talk very loudly, only eat fast food and wear colourful clothes.
- why you think the stereotype exists.
  I think it's because some American tourists in Britain are a bit like that sometimes, and in some films, too.
- why this stereotype is wrong.
  My friend went to the US last year. She said she ate excellent food and the Americans she met were quiet and stylishly dressed!

DEVELOPING SPEAKING

1 7.04 **Look at the photo. How do you think the people feel about each other? Listen and read to check.**

Jackie: Well, I think you're being unfair. Just because he likes different music from you ...

Luke: It's not just that and you know it! Harry's boring and there's no way I want him there.

Mum: Pack it in, you two. Please! I'm tired of this endless arguing. What is it now? Let me guess. It's who you're going to invite.

Jackie: Got it in one, Mum. The thing is, we haven't got the same friends, so it's hard when we're having just one party!

Luke: I'm with Jackie on this one, Mum. Can't we have two parties?

Mum: How is that going to work? You're twins, so your birthdays are on the same day. And we live in one house. One house, one day, one party. You can invite thirty people – end of story.

Jackie: So, Luke, we've got to find a way to do this. Don't get me wrong, but I think you could be more ... well, flexible, you know? I know you don't like Harry, but can't you get along with him for one evening?

Mum: Good point, Jackie.

Luke: Well, I suppose you're right.

Jackie: And listen, I promise you can invite Mary Tanner and I won't complain. OK?

Mum: That's more like it. A little bit of give-and-take.

Luke: Thanks for helping us sort it, Mum.

Mum: Don't mention it. Now, let's all go out and buy some decorations.

2 7.04 **Listen and read the dialogue again. Answer the questions.**

1 Why can't Luke and Jackie have separate parties?
2 What does Jackie say Luke should try to do?
3 How does Jackie feel about Mary Tanner?
4 Who is going to buy decorations?

3 SPEAKING **Discuss the statements in pairs. What do you think?**

1 Luke and Jackie should have their parties on two different days.
2 Jackie's right to ask Luke to be nice to Harry.
3 Their mother sorts out their problem.

Phrases for fluency

4 **Find the underlined expressions in the dialogue. How do you say them in your language?**

5 **Replace each underlined part with an expression from the dialogue.**

1 A Thanks for your help.
  B You're welcome.
2 A If we don't leave now, we'll be late.
  B Yes, I think you're right. Let's go!
3 A You look happy. Good exam results?
  B You're right immediately! I got 95%.
4 A Dad, Alex won't let me use the computer.
  B Arguing again? Stop it now before I get angry!
5 A You're always looking at your phone. Don't misunderstand me, but I think you should use it less.
6 A It's raining. I suggest we watch a film inside.
  B I agree with you. Which film shall we watch?

FUNCTIONS
Invitations

KEY LANGUAGE

Making invitations
Why don't you (join us)? / How about (coming with us)? Do you fancy (going to the cinema with me)?

Accepting invitations
That'd be (great). / I'd love to. / Yes, of course, thank you.

Declining an invitation
Sorry, I can't. / You'll have to count me out.

6 **Complete the sentences with the words in the list.**

about	count	course	
don't	fancy	love	would

1 Why ______________ you come along?
2 How ______________ bringing some friends along with you?
3 Do you ______________ coming along?
4 That ______________ be fantastic. I'd ______________ to.
5 Yes, of ______________. It's a great idea.
6 You'll have to ______________ me out.

ROLE PLAY **Work in pairs. Student A: turn to page 127. Student B: turn to page 128.**

PRONUNCIATION
Intonation – inviting, accepting and refusing invitations Go to page 121.

LIFE COMPETENCIES

Getting along with others is important. We don't always agree with other people or like the way they do things. However, even when we disagree with them, we ought to be friendly and respect them.

1 ▶ 19 **Watch the vlog. How would you describe the situation at home between Leo and his sister?**

2 ▶ 19 **Watch the vlog again and make notes on:**

a three annoying things Leo does.

b three annoying things his sister does.

3 **Compare your notes with a partner.**

4 **Read the situations. Make notes about what you would do in each situation.**

A You are working on a project with a group of students in your class. You have lots of good ideas that you want to use, but one person is difficult to work with. She also has lots of ideas for the project, but the problem is you don't think her ideas are very good. She says that you are too bossy and that you won't listen to anyone else, because you think your ideas are the best.

B You have always been good at English, in particular creative writing, and you usually get top marks. You used to have a good relationship with your teacher, but recently, he has started to be quite negative about your work and has even criticised it in front of the class. Last week, you got a really bad mark for your homework and you don't know why. When you tried to speak to your teacher about it, he seemed annoyed.

5 **Compare your answers with a partner. Do you agree? Have you ever been in a similar situation? What did you do?**

6 SPEAKING **Work in pairs. Match the solutions 1–4 to situations A and B in Exercise 4. Then discuss. Which solutions do you think are the best? Which would you *not* recommend?**

1 Suggest everyone in the group votes on which ideas to use. Both of you will have to be prepared to accept that it may not be your ideas that are chosen.

2 Confront your teacher again and ask for an explanation. Explain that your work won't improve unless he gives you clear feedback on exactly what the problem is. Refuse to leave until it is resolved.

3 Listen to your friend's ideas and think about how they could work with your own. Maybe you could use some of your ideas and some of hers, too.

4 Try talking to another teacher. Ask him/her for advice on how to deal with the situation.

Me and my world

7 **Think of someone you don't get along well with. Write down:**

1 three reasons why you don't get along.

2 three things you could do to change things.

TIPS FOR GETTING ALONG WITH OTHERS

- **Take a bit of time to stop and think about what someone has said or done. Don't respond or react in anger. This could make the situation worse.**
- **Be positive. Think of solutions to your problem before you speak to the person.**
- **Try to feel empathy. There may be a reason why the person is behaving a certain way. Ask how they are feeling.**

8 CRIME AND PUNISHMENT

Get THINKING

Watch the video and think:
do you always pay for the music you listen to?

OBJECTIVES

FUNCTIONS:
reporting what someone said, asked or requested; giving and reacting to news

GRAMMAR:
reported speech (review); reported questions, requests and imperatives

VOCABULARY:
crime; reporting verbs

READING

1 **Look at the words for different types of criminals. How do you say them in your language?**

1 burglar	3 poacher	5 robber
2 con man	4 pickpocket	6 shoplifter

2 **Match the pictures with words from Exercise 1.**

3 **Think of examples of these criminals from the news, books, TV or films.**

4 8.01 **Look at the photos and headlines on the next page. Guess what the news stories are about. Then read and listen to check.**

5 **Read the news stories again. In which stories do these things happen? Write *lion* or *rhino*.**

1 The criminals tried to get rid of the evidence. ______
2 The criminals were caught as they tried to kill the animal. ______
3 The criminals attacked the agents. ______
4 The criminals were caught after a car chase. ______
5 It was not the first time the criminals had got into trouble. ______
6 The agents found important evidence among the criminals' possessions. ______
7 The criminals are facing charges for three different crimes. ______
8 Agents believe their work is starting to make a difference. ______

Train to THINK

Thinking about empathy

To understand another person's feelings, you need to 'put yourself in their shoes' – try to imagine how you'd feel in their situation.

6 **Read the first story again. Who do you think felt these emotions? Match 1–2 with a–b.**

1 the agents ☐
2 the poachers ☐

a excitement and pride
b regret and guilt

7 **Why do you think they might have felt these things? What other emotions do you think they might feel?**

8 **How do these stories make you feel? Tell your partner.**

CRIMES!

POACHERS *ARRESTED*

Anti-poaching agents in Limpopo, South Africa caught two poachers as they tried to kill lions at the Letaba River Wildlife Reserve Park last Sunday evening.

The agents had received information about the planned attack and made plans of their own to catch the criminals in the act.

Under a full moon, the poachers broke into the park where the agents were waiting. They jumped on the poachers as they approached the cages where the lions were kept for their own protection. After a short fight, in which one of the poachers used a knife, the agents were able to arrest the two men.

One of the agents said that they had searched the men's rucksacks and had found poisoned dead chickens and wire cutting equipment. He explained how poachers throw the chickens to the lions, wait for the lions to eat the chickens, and then return when the animals are dead. He also said that the poachers could sell the dead animals for over $3,500.

The poachers are now in jail awaiting trial. The prisoners are facing charges of attempted poaching, possession of a dangerous weapon and attempted murder. If found guilty, they could go to prison for up to ten years. An anti-poaching agent said he hoped this would be a warning to other poachers and help in their fight against one of their country's most serious problems.

CAUGHT *RED-HANDED*

In another part of Limpopo, three rhino horn smugglers have been caught red-handed by members of the Limpopo Endangered Species Unit. The agents had received information the men were trying to sell the illegal item. As they approached the men's car, it drove away quickly and a large item was thrown from the window. While one agent got the item, which turned out to be the horn, others chased and caught the three men. Two of the men, who are brothers, were already known to the agents. They had been arrested in 2014 for rhino poaching but had not been sent to prison and were let go. This time agents are hoping they will finally be sent to prison. They believe the horn comes from a rhino that was shot dead a week ago in a nearby area. Agents said they were going to send the horn for testing to see if they are right.

Rhino poaching continues to be a huge problem in many southern African countries as the demand for their horns increases around the world. But South African law officers are determined to protect the animals and are spending more money to catch those committing the crimes. An official from the department of environmental affairs said that the situation was improving and that the number of rhino deaths in 2016 had fallen since the record number of over 1,200 in 2014. They also said they are using modern technology in their fight. One technique is to put a dye into the rhino's horns, which is poisonous for humans but perfectly safe for the rhinos.

SPEAKING

9 SPEAKING **Work in pairs. Discuss these questions.**

1 What punishment do you think these men should get?

2 What other animals do you know that are in danger from poachers?

GRAMMAR
Reported speech (review)

1 Complete the sentences with suitable verbs. Then check your answers in the news stories on page 75.

1 One of the agents said that they ______________ the men's rucksacks.
2 He also said the poachers ______________ the dead animals for over $3,500.
3 An anti-poaching agent said that he ______________ this ______________ be a warning to other poachers.
4 Agents said they ______________ the horn for testing.
5 An official from the department of environmental affairs said that the situation ______________ .
6 He said that the number of rhino deaths in 2016 ______________ since the record number of over 1,200 in 2014.

2 Match what was said (direct speech) with the reported sentences in Exercise 1. Underline the verb forms which are different. Then complete the rule.

a 'We're going to send the horn for testing.'
b 'I hope this will be a warning to other poachers.'
c 'The number of rhino deaths in 2016 has fallen since the record number of over 1,200 in 2014.'
d 'The poachers can sell the dead animals for over $3,500.'
e 'We searched their rucksacks.'
f 'The situation is improving.'

RULE:

Direct speech		Reported speech
present simple	→	0 *past simple*
present continuous	→	1 ______________
present perfect	→	2 ______________
past simple	→	3 ______________
past perfect	→	*past perfect*
would	→	*would*
can	→	4 ______________
will	→	5 ______________
am/ is / are going to	→	6 ______________

3 Rewrite these sentences in reported speech.

1 'I'll be happy to put cameras all over the park,' the manager said.
2 'The agents can't wait for the DNA report,' the reporter said.
3 'We saw the men from across the street,' the woman told the police.
4 'We're thinking of having a new alarm installed,' the manager said.
5 'We haven't done anything,' one of the brothers said.
6 'You'll get a long time in jail for this,' the agent told the poachers.

→ workbook page 72

VOCABULARY
Crime

4 Match the words with the definitions.

murder | break in | arrest | a fine
commit a crime | go to prison | a murderer
get into trouble | get caught | a prisoner

1 to do something illegal
2 to be made to live in a special building for criminals
3 to take (a suspected criminal) to the police station
4 to kill (a person) intentionally
5 money that you have to pay if you break a law
6 to enter by force (usually to steal something)
7 someone who intentionally kills another person
8 to be found while committing a crime
9 to have a problem because of something that you did wrong
10 a person who is in prison

5 SPEAKING Work in pairs. Use these questions to help you invent a crime story. Make notes and then tell your partner your story.

- Where and when did it happen?
- Who was involved?
- What happened?
- What crime was committed?
- How did the police react?
- What happened to the criminal?

→ workbook page 74

LISTENING

6 SPEAKING **Imagine a young person mugged somebody. Discuss these questions.**

1 Why might someone mug a person?
2 Who might suffer as a result?
3 What would be the best punishment?

7 8.02 **Listen to a radio interview. What is Restoring Justice and who is it for?**

8 8.02 **Listen again and make notes on these topics.**

1 Jason's initial reaction to Restoring Justice
2 the main idea behind Restoring Justice
3 how Jason felt about meeting his victim
4 how Mrs Schwartz felt about meeting her mugger
5 the reason Jason gave for mugging Mrs Schwartz
6 the people Mrs Schwartz feels suffered most

GRAMMAR

Reported questions, requests and imperatives

9 Match 1–4 with a–d. Then complete the rule with *asked*, *if*, *told* and *whether*.

1 She asked me if I knew who'd suffered ☐
2 [The judge] asked me whether I wanted ☐
3 [She] asked me to look at the other side ☐
4 He told me to ☐

a think carefully about my choices.
b to go to prison.
c of the table, where my mum and dad were sitting.
d most from what I'd done.

RULE:
- In reported *yes / no* questions, we use *asked* + [5] _______ or _______ and the same word order as in a statement.
- In reported requests, we use [6] _______ + object + infinitive.
- In reported imperatives, we use [7] _______ + object + infinitive.

10 These are things people have said to Ken, the social worker. Rewrite them in reported speech.

0 Reporter: 'Have you had much success with the programme so far?'
The reporter asked if he'd had much success with the programme so far.
1 Presenter: 'Are victims scared of meeting their muggers?'
2 Ken's wife: 'Did you see the article about Restoring Justice in the newspaper this morning?'
3 Presenter: 'Could you tell us more about the ideas behind the programme, please?'
4 Ken's manager: 'Don't include other criminals in the programme.'

11 Write four to six more questions that Mrs Schwartz might ask Jason. Use direct speech. Then put your partner's questions into reported speech.

'How do you see your future?'
She asked him how he saw his future.

→ workbook page 72

TH!NK values

Respecting the law

12 Match the punishments (1–6) with the sentences (a–f).

1 He got a fine. ☐
2 He got community service. ☐
3 He got a life sentence. ☐
4 He got a caution. ☐
5 He got the death penalty. ☐
6 He got a prison sentence. ☐

a He has to spend 80 hours cleaning the streets.
b But he'll be in serious trouble if he does it again.
c It means at least 20 years in prison.
d But it will be years before they carry it out.
e He had to pay £100.
f He'll be inside for two years.

13 Number the punishments in Exercise 12 from 1 (least serious) to 6 (most serious).

14 SPEAKING **Work in pairs. Read these newspaper headlines. What crimes have been committed? What punishment (if any) would be fair?**

- Hungry student steals chocolate bar from shop
- Man steals TV from old couple's home
- Speeding driver kills family of four
- Bank robber escapes with thousands

READING

1 **Read the article quickly. What do these numbers refer to?**

a 16%   b 25%   c 361   d 78   e 250

EATING OUT

BEHIND BARS

Next time you're looking for a special evening out, why not invite someone special to eat out with you at one of the Clink restaurants? They offer delicious, beautifully cooked dishes, but this is fine dining with a difference, because these are no ordinary restaurants. The Clink restaurants are found inside four of the UK's most famous prisons; High Down, Brixton, Cardiff and Styal, so your waiter might be a burglar and your food might have been cooked by a robber. Because the restaurants are actually inside the prison walls, anyone wanting to eat out in one of the Clink prisons has to agree to go through a special security check first.

The man behind the idea is Chef Alberto Crisci, who was looking for a way to help prisoners make the most of their time inside by studying for professional cooking qualifications. He also wanted to offer members of the public a chance to eat out somewhere truly different, so he set up the Clink charity to make all this happen. The idea is to encourage prisoners to learn how to do a new job while they are in prison. When they are released from prison with their newly earned qualifications, they can persuade restaurant owners to give them a job. It is hoped that then they will be less likely to commit crimes in the future.

Supporters of the restaurants claim that it really works. They explain that only 16% of prisoners who have worked in the Clink restaurants commit crimes in the year after they are released – compared to the national average of 25% of adult prisoners. Some critics refuse to accept these figures. They say that only the prisoners who are likely not to return to crime are chosen to work in the restaurants. But the organisers of the charity are not worried by this argument. They have plenty more evidence to show how successful they are. In 2018, 361 prisoners were trained in the Clink restaurants and 142 earned a professional qualification; 78 out of 112 ex-prisoners who had worked in Clink found jobs on release and 250 restaurants said they were happy to take on graduates from the training programme. One graduate even made a successful appearance on the TV cookery show *Bake Off: The Professionals*.

So if you're looking for a great meal out and like the idea of helping a criminal make a new start, one of the Clink restaurants might just be the place you're looking for. But I'd recommend that you book early. The restaurants are extremely popular.

2 8.03 **Read and listen to the article and mark the sentences T (true) or F (false).**

1 The food in the Clink restaurants is not particularly good. ☐
2 Alberto Crisci wanted to improve the quality of meals in prisons. ☐
3 You can't just walk into a Clink restaurant. ☐
4 Prisoners with Clink qualifications are less likely than other prisoners to go back to prison. ☐
5 Not everyone agrees that the programme is really successful. ☐
6 It's easy to get a table at one of the Clink restaurants. ☐

3 SPEAKING **Work in pairs. Discuss these questions.**

1 Would you like to visit a Clink restaurant? Why (not)?
2 What other useful skills could prisoners learn in prison?

VOCABULARY
Reporting verbs

4 Complete the sentences with the correct forms of the verbs. Then check your answers in the article on page 78.

agree | claim | encourage | explain | invite
persuade | recommend | refuse

1 Supporters of the restaurant ______ that it works.
2 They ______ that only 16% of prisoners who have worked in the Clink restaurants commit crimes in the year after they are released.
3 Anyone wanting to eat out in one of the Clink prisons has to ______ to go through a special security check first.
4 Why not ______ someone special to eat out with you at one of the Clink restaurants?
5 I'd ______ that you book early.
6 Some critics ______ to accept these figures.
7 The idea is to ______ prisoners to learn how to do a new job.
8 They can ______ restaurant owners to give them a job.

5 Match the verbs (1–5) with the definitions (a–e).

1 agree ☐
2 claim ☐
3 explain ☐
4 persuade ☐
5 refuse ☐

a make something clear
b try to get someone to do or believe something
c accept an idea or a suggestion
d say no
e say that something is true

6 Complete the rule with reporting verbs from Exercises 4 and 5. Some verbs can go in more than one list.

RULE:
We use different structures with different reporting verbs.
1 verb + infinitive with (*not*) *to agree, offer*, ______ , ______
2 verb + object + infinitive with (*not*) *to ask, tell*, ______ , ______ , ______
3 verb + *that* + clause *say, claim*, ______ , ______ , ______
4 verb + gerund *apologise for, suggest*, ______

7 Complete the sentences with the correct forms of the verbs and any other necessary words.

1 Liam agreed ______ (meet) me at nine o'clock.
2 Lucy apologised ______ (forget) my birthday.
3 Jack refused ______ (help) us.
4 Bobby persuaded ______ (me / go) to the party with him.
5 Dad suggested ______ (have) dinner at a restaurant.
6 My mum encouraged ______ (me / enter) the singing competition.
7 Mr Jones recommended ______ (we / read) the book before we saw the film.
8 Liz offered ______ (drive) me home after the match.

8 Rewrite the sentences in reported speech. Use suitable reporting verbs. Sometimes more than one verb is possible.

1 'We forgot to inform you. We're really sorry,' they said.
2 'We're going to introduce a new system to reduce crime,' the mayor said.
3 'Can you give us more information about the plan?' the reporter said to the official.
4 'If you work for us, you'll be very rich soon,' the man said.
5 'I don't want to buy the watch because it's too expensive,' the woman said.
6 'Study this text carefully!' the teacher said to the class.
7 'I can help you with your work,' the man said.
8 'Come to my office tomorrow morning, please,' the headmaster said to my parents.
9 'Oh, all right. I'll go to the cinema with you, but only if you pay,' Jack said to Olivia.

→ workbook page 74

WRITING
A report of a crime

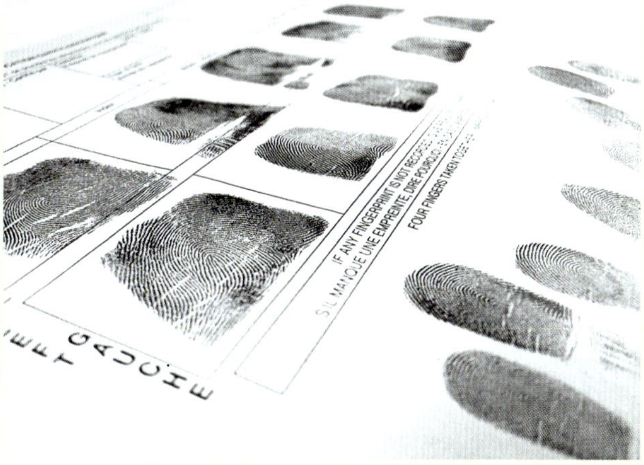

9 Write a newspaper report about a crime (100–150 words).

- Give a description of the crime (what happened).
- Include what one witness said.
- Say what the investigators think.

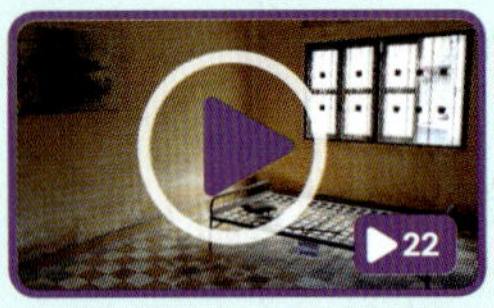

TH!NK

Famous prisons

Culture

1 Scan the article and find one famous prisoner from each prison.

2 🔊 8.04 Read and listen to the article to check your answers.

FAMOUS PRISONS

1 ROBBEN ISLAND, SOUTH AFRICA

Robben Island is known all over the world because of one of its former prisoners. From 1964 until 1982 this island prison, 11km off the coast of Cape Town, was home to perhaps the most famous prisoner in the world, Nelson Mandela, who in 1994 became the first black president of his country. Robben Island was used mainly for political prisoners and more than 3,000 of them spent time there before it was finally closed in 1996. These days it is a museum and it is visited by thousands of tourists each year.

2 ALCATRAZ, US

Another island that was home to a prison is Alcatraz, which is situated 2km off the coast of San Francisco. Probably America's most well-known prison, Alcatraz had many famous inmates, such as the gangster Al Capone and Robert 'Birdman' Stroud, a murderer who was also one of the country's biggest experts on birds. Alcatraz closed in 1963 and in its 29 years of being a prison, no one ever escaped, although 36 prisoners tried. These days it is open to the public and tourists can take a short boat journey across the San Francisco bay to visit it.

3 THE TOWER OF LONDON, UK

The Tower of London, which was built in the 11th century, is now one of the city's most popular tourist attractions, with people coming from all over the world to see the Crown Jewels that are kept inside it. However, up until the mid 20th century, it was a prison and home to many famous prisoners, including King Henry VI and two of King Henry VIII's wives, Anne Boleyn and Catherine Howard, who were also both executed in the Tower. Visitors see the cells and enjoy interactive displays that show what life was like in this ancient prison.

4 CHÂTEAU D'IF, FRANCE

Although Château d'If is a real island, most people know of it because of a fictional prisoner. The island prison, which is situated off the coast of Marseilles in the south of France, was home to many criminals from the mid 17th century to the end of the 19th century, but it is really famous for one prisoner who was never actually there. In his novel *The Count of Monte Cristo*, French author Alexandre Dumas tells the story of Edmond Dantès, an innocent man who is sent to the prison for a crime he did not commit. In the book, Dantès manages to escape, something that no prisoner was ever able to do in real life.

5 DEVIL'S ISLAND, FRENCH GUIANA

Devil's Island is off the coast of French Guiana in the Caribbean. For the hundred years that it was open, it was known as one of the toughest prisons in the world and fewer than 25% of all prisoners who went there left the island alive. The prison was set in the middle of a jungle and the waters around it were full of man-eating sharks, which made escape almost impossible. One man who managed to escape and write a book about his experiences was Henri Charrière and the film *Papillon* tells his story. Since it was closed in 1953, Devil's Island has become a tourist attraction for passengers on the many cruise ships that pass nearby.

3 **Answer the questions.**

According to the texts, which prison or prisons …

1 was impossible to escape from?
2 was home to a future politician?
3 can now be visited by members of the public?
4 is not on an island?
5 contains really valuable objects?
6 appeared in a book?

4 SPEAKING **Work in pairs. Discuss these questions.**

1 What other famous prisons do you know of either in real life or in films/books?
2 Would you like to visit any of these prisons? Why or why not?

5 VOCABULARY There are eight highlighted words or phrases in the article. Match the words with these meanings. Write the words.

1 rooms in prison where prisoners are kept
2 killed as a legal punishment
3 valuable stones
4 place visited by people on holiday
5 at an earlier time
6 people who know a lot about something
7 not guilty
8 people who are kept in prison

LISTENING

6 8.05 Listen to the conversations and match them with the photos.

A

B

C

D

7 8.05 Listen again and complete the notes.

Conversation 1

Criminal: ______ What was taken: ______

Conversation 2

Criminal: ______ What was taken: ______

Conversation 3

Criminal: ______ What was taken: ______

Conversation 4

Criminal: ______ What was taken: ______

FUNCTIONS

Giving and reacting to news

8 Put the words in order to form expressions for giving news from the conversations.

1 never / You'll / what / guess
2 believe / won't / to / week / what / You / happened / last / me
3 about / a / really / an / sad / lady / story / heard / I / old
4 paper / a / scary / story / There / the / was / other / in / day / the

9 Complete the reactions to news.

1 T _ ll m _ .
2 Wh _ t?
3 R _ _ lly?
4 Th _ t's _ wf _ l!
5 N _ w _ y!

10 SPEAKING Work in pairs. Make conversations using the expressions from Exercises 8 and 9.

- Think of (or make up) a piece of news.
- Take turns to give your news.
- React and ask for more details.

PRONUNCIATION
Intonation – expressing surprise
Go to page 121.

TOWARDS B2 First for Schools

READING AND USE OF ENGLISH

Word formation

→ workbook page 71

1 **For questions 1–7, read the text below. Use the word given in capitals at the end of some of the lines to form a word that fits in the gap in the same line. There is an example at the beginning (0).**

A thief who kissed his victim after a [0] *robbery* in a	**ROB**
French jewellery shop has been caught after a forensic	
[1] __________ matched his DNA with that left on the	**SCIENCE**
hand of his victim.	
The thief [2] __________ the Parisian shop late in the	**ENTRY**
afternoon, as the owner was preparing to close for the	
evening. After tying the woman to a chair, he smashed	
open [3] __________ display cabinets and loaded	**VARY**
[4] __________ worth more than 20,000 euros into	**VALUE**
a bag. Before leaving the shop, he kissed the owner's	
hand and made an [5] __________ for his crime.	**APOLOGISE**
However, the [6] __________ thief could never have	**LUCK**
imagined that the kiss would lead to his arrest.	
Police used the DNA and ran it through a	
database of all known [7] __________ .	**CRIME**

WRITING

An informal email

→ workbook page 79

2 **You have received an email from an English-speaking penfriend.**

To: Mike
mike_2000@mail.com

Subject: Any suggestions?

Hey Mike,

How are things? Listen, I'm writing because a friend of mine is coming to spend a few days in your town. She asked me to write to you to see if you could suggest some of the things she should do while she's there. She also wanted to know what the weather's like and what clothes she should bring with her. She leaves on Friday. Sorry for the short notice, but can you help?

Hope to hear from you soon.

Best,

Angie

Write your email in 140–190 words.

TEST YOURSELF UNITS 7 & 8

VOCABULARY

1 Complete the sentences with the words / phrases in the list. There are four extra words / phrases.

give up | got into trouble | unfriendly | generous | find out | after all
commit a crime | polite | selfish | set off | burglar | shy | arrested | end up

1 Don't ______________________ now. You're a great player. I'm sure you'll get on the team next time.
2 That was very ______________________ of you to eat all those cakes and not leave any for us.
3 We ______________________ very early in the morning because we wanted to arrive before it got dark.
4 Tim ______________________ for not doing his English homework again.
5 The ______________________ broke into the house when everybody was asleep.
6 I hope they ______________________ who stole Amanda's purse.
7 It was very ______________________ of James to pay for all your concert tickets.
8 It rained a lot that day, so we didn't go on the school trip ______________________ .
9 The police finally ______________________ the con man and he went to prison.
10 Emma's very ______________________ . She always says 'please' and 'thank you'.

/10

GRAMMAR

2 Complete the sentences with the words / phrases in the list. There are two extra words / phrases.

get used to | would | 'm not used to | going to | encouraged | is | had been | got used to

1 My mum ______________________ me to do well at school.
2 The policeman told me that the robber ______________________ get a prison sentence.
3 I ______________________ taking my shoes off before I go into a house, but here in Japan, it's what everyone does.
4 She says she is ______________________ report the crime to the police.
5 At home, I always have dinner at six o'clock, so I haven't ______________________ eating at nine o'clock here in Spain.
6 She said the con man ______________________ sentenced to two years in prison.

3 Find and correct the mistake in each sentence.

1 She asked me if I knew who has taken the bike.
2 My mum let me do all the washing-up for a week because I was late home one night.
3 He persuaded me report the incident to the police.
4 I really want to go on the school trip, but my dad won't make me.
5 The reporter explained me that the mugger would get community service.
6 My parents make me to tidy my bedroom.

/12

FUNCTIONAL LANGUAGE

4 Choose the correct words.

1 A We're going camping this weekend. Why don't you come *along* / *on*?
B I'd love to. How *for* / *about* asking Mike to come, too?
2 A We're going swimming. Does anyone *feel* / *fancy* joining us?
B You can *call* / *count* me out. I hate swimming.
3 A The other day I *hear* / *heard* a really sad story about an old man whose house was burgled.
B *That's* / *It's* awful.
4 A You'll never *believe* / *understand* what happened to me last week!
B Go on then. *Say* / *Tell* me!

/8

MY SCORE /30

22–30 | 10–21 | 0–9

9 IT'S A MYSTERY!

Get THINKING

Watch the video and think: are there any unexplained mysteries from your country?

OBJECTIVES

FUNCTIONS: making deductions

GRAMMAR: modals of deduction (present); *should(n't) have*; modals of deduction (past)

VOCABULARY: mysteries; expressions with *go*

A

C

B

D

READING

1 **Look at the photos and match them with the mysteries.**

1 Stonehenge | **2** the Loch Ness Monster
3 the yeti | **4** UFOs

2 SPEAKING **Work in pairs. Compare your answers. What do you know about these mysteries?**

3 **Read the article on the next page quickly. Why *isn't* the author writing about any of the mysteries in Exercise 1?**

4 9.01 **Read and listen to the article. Write B (balls), O (octopuses), S (spaceman) or V (Voynich) in the boxes to answer the questions.**

Which mystery …

1 is about the appearance of a mysterious character? ☐
2 is about things that were difficult to make? ☐
3 is a challenge to language experts? ☐
4 is about the unusual behaviour of some creatures? ☐
5 involves huge stone objects? ☐
6 involves a book written centuries ago? ☐
7 can perhaps be explained by the weather? ☐
8 is about a family and a photograph? ☐

Train to THINK

Fact or opinion?

A fact is something that can be proven to be true.

An opinion is a personal belief. It's important to be able to see the difference.

5 **Read about the octopuses again. According to what is written in the text, mark the sentences F (fact) or O (opinion).**

1 The population of the octopuses is bigger now than before. ☐
2 The octopuses needed to travel to find food. ☐
3 There were storms not long before they were seen walking on the beach. ☐
4 The octopuses had a disease. ☐

6 **Complete the table with two facts and two opinions for each mystery according to the article.**

	Facts	Opinions
1 Giant stone balls		
2 Solway spaceman		
3 Voynich manuscript		

THE TRUTH IS OUT THERE

There are many unexplained mysteries in the world. How was the Great Pyramid at Giza built? Are there yetis in the Himalayas? Is there a monster in the depths of Loch Ness? Here are our favourites.

A The octopuses that walked on land

You might see an octopus hop from one rock pool to another, but in late October 2017, over 20 octopuses were seen coming out of the sea and moving along a beach in Wales. 'No one has ever seen anything like this before,' said one local. 'It's very odd behaviour.' So, why did it happen? Different experts have different opinions. One is that the octopuses were ill. Another is that two big storms a few days earlier had confused the octopuses and affected their senses. A third expert said: 'There's been an increase in the octopus population, so it might be the octopuses needed to travel further to find food.'

B The giant stone balls

There are hundreds of large stone balls in the Costa Rican jungle. Evidence shows that they must be at least 600 years old and some could date back to 200 BCE. The spheres are up to 2.4 metres in diameter and are almost perfectly round. They are also very heavy, with some of them weighing 16 tons. The stone itself comes from miles away, so it took a huge effort to move them. It's thought they probably had a religious purpose and some people suggest a connection with the sun. Others have even suggested that the balls were created by an alien life form. But no one really knows and the mystery continues.

C The Solway spaceman

In 1964, Jim Templeton from Carlisle took a photo of his daughter Elizabeth and was surprised to see in the photo a strange figure behind her that looked like an extraterrestrial spaceman. Jim took the photo with the mysterious figure to the police, and soon afterwards it appeared in the newspapers. Then one day, Jim was visited by two men who said they were government officials. They asked him to take them to the scene of the photograph. Who were they? Why were they interested? Some people say the figure in the photo must be Templeton's wife – the camera flash made her dress look bright white. Most people agree that the image is real but can't be a spaceman. What do you think?

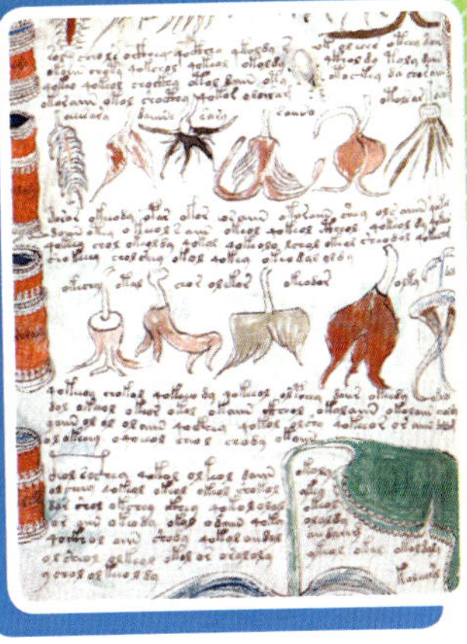

D The Voynich manuscript

In 1639, Georgius Barschius from Prague told a friend that he had a mysterious book which might be about science or medicine. It was full of puzzling pictures and diagrams, and it was written in an unknown language. Today, the Voynich manuscript is over 600 years old and still no one can read it. It has been suggested that the mysterious writing could be based on an Arabic or Roma or Aztec language. Others say it must be a secret code, and many expert codebreakers have tried to crack it. Every year people think they have solved the mystery, but no one ever has.

SPEAKING

7 Work in pairs. Discuss these questions.

1 Which of these mysteries do you think is the most interesting? Why?
2 What other mysteries do you know of?

PRONUNCIATION
Moving word stress Go to page 121.

GRAMMAR

Modals of deduction (present)

1 Complete the sentences from the article on page 85. Use *must, can't, could* and *might*. Then complete the rule.

1 You ______ see an octopus hop from one rock pool to another.
2 Some of the giant stone balls ______ date back to 200 BCE.
3 Most people agree that the image ______ be a spaceman.
4 Others say that it ______ be a secret code.

> **RULE:**
> When we're sure something is true, we use [5] ______ .
> When we're sure something isn't true, we use [6] ______ .
> When we think something is possibly true, but aren't sure, we use [7] ______ or ______ .

2 Complete the sentences with suitable modal verbs. Sometimes there's more than one possible answer.

1 They're speaking Spanish, so they ______ be from Argentina, I suppose.
2 She ______ love cats – she's got 20.
3 You ______ want more – you've already eaten two whole pizzas!
4 I'm not sure, but I think that man ______ need our help. I don't think he can swim.
5 You've been working all day. You ______ feel really tired.
6 He's a bit older than John, but he ______ know him. I think they went to the same school.
7 Tim ______ be happy. He studied really hard, but he still failed the test.
8 It's the world's oldest mystery. You ______ know the answer.

→ workbook page 82

VOCABULARY

Mysteries

3 Add the missing vowels to make adjectives related to mysteries.

1 _ n _ x p l _ _ n _ d mysteries
2 _ d d behaviour
3 _ l _ _ n life form
4 s t r _ n g _ figure
5 _ x t r _ t _ r r _ s t r _ _ l spaceman
6 m y s t _ r _ _ _ s writing
7 p _ z z l _ n g pictures
8 a s _ c r _ t code

4 Answer the questions about the words from Exercise 3.

1 Which two words mean 'from another world'?
2 Which word means 'known by very few people'?

5 Complete the text with the adjectives from Exercise 3.

I left for school at the usual time, but something seemed wrong. The streets were empty and there was a [1]m ______ feeling in the air. I passed a few people, but they all seemed rather [2]o ______ . I didn't see anyone from school on the way. When I got to school, the gates were closed. Why were they closed? I looked at my watch – 9 am. The gates should be open. This was most [3]p ______ .

I pushed the gates open and walked inside. Where was everyone? Had they been transported away by some [4]e ______ beings and taken to an [5]a ______ planet? Had they all been taken away as part of some [6]s ______ government experiment? What should I do? Run away? No, this was one mystery that couldn't be left [7]u ______ . I had to find out where everyone was.

I opened the school door and walked inside. I saw a man – it was Mr Barnes, who looked after the school. I ran up to him. 'Thank goodness!' I cried. 'Where is everyone?' He gave me a [8]s ______ look.

'At home, probably,' he replied. 'It's Saturday morning.'

→ workbook page 84

LISTENING

6 Match the pictures with the words.

1 fortune-teller 2 rope 3 housekeeper 4 chandelier

7 9.04 **Listen to a story called *The Case of the Mysterious Fall*. Why is the fall mysterious?**

8 9.04 **Listen again. Mark the sentences T (true), F (false) or DS (doesn't say).**

1 Mr Huntingdon was friendly and sociable. ☐
2 He only spoke to one person each week. ☐
3 He thought of a plan to try and cheat death. ☐
4 Mr Huntingdon tried to call Mrs Crabtree back to the house after she'd left. ☐
5 Mrs Crabtree always started work at 8 am. ☐
6 The fortune-teller's prediction came true. ☐

GRAMMAR

should(n't) have

9 Look at these sentences from the listening. Answer the questions. Then complete the rule.

1 Maybe [Mrs Crabtree] should have asked why.
  a Did Mrs Crabtree ask why?
  b Would it have been a good idea to?
2 He shouldn't have sent Mrs Crabtree home.
  a Did Mr Huntingdon send Mrs Crabtree home?
  b Was it a good idea to?

> RULE: To criticise actions in the past, we use *should* / *shouldn't* + [3]______ + the [4]______ form of the verb.

10 Write replies to the statements. Use *should have* or *shouldn't have* and suitable verbs. Then practise reading them out in pairs.

0 'I had five slices of pizza! Now I feel sick.'
  'You shouldn't have eaten so much pizza!'
1 'We've broken the TV. Quick! Put the ball away!'
2 'I bought these jeans yesterday, but now I haven't got enough money to buy Mum a birthday present.'
3 'I failed the test!'
4 'Joey didn't invite me to his party.'
5 'You only paid 100 for those tickets? I paid 250!'

11 SPEAKING **Work in pairs. Write three sentences about famous people using *should have* or *shouldn't have*. Then read them out without saying the names. Your partner tries to guess who the people are.**

→ workbook page 82

THINK *values*

Thinking carefully before you act

12 SPEAKING **Work in pairs. Which do you think was Mr Huntingdon's biggest mistake?**

A He should have thought about his plan more carefully.
B He should have told Mrs Crabtree about the fortune-teller's prediction.
C He shouldn't have gone to see the fortune-teller.

13 SPEAKING **Look at the pictures. What mistake did each person make? What should they have done?**

READING

1 SPEAKING Look at the pictures. What do you see in them? Discuss your answers in pairs.

2 9.05 Read and listen to the article. Why do you think the photo of the dress went viral?

3 Read the article again. Find and match 1–6 with a–f.

1 ☐ started a family argument
2 ☐ sold the dress
3 ☐ became an internet sensation
4 ☐ set up a study
5 ☐ studied the photo
6 ☐ makes decisions about colours

a the brain
b researchers
c scientists
d the retailer
e the dress
f the photo of the dress

THE DRESS

It goes without saying that people love optical illusions – they've always been popular in books and pictures. Now, with social media, we've gone one step further and everyone is sharing these puzzling illusions. Here's one that really went down a storm with people all round the world.

Is it blue and black, **or** white and gold? Which two colours would you go for? This is the story of how an ordinary dress became an internet sensation. You can't have missed it!

The mother of a bride sent her daughter a photo of a dress that she was planning to wear to the wedding and it started an argument between the daughter, her fiancé and their friends. Some of them saw the dress as white and gold while others saw it as blue and black. How weird is that?

One friend posted the photo on the internet and the social media world went crazy. Within a week, the photo went viral and more than 10 million tweets mentioned the dress, using hashtags such as #thedress, #whiteandgold and #blueandblack. The retailer confirmed that the actual colour of the dress was blue and black, but the debate went on.

So why did people see the dress so differently? After reviewing the photo, scientists had some answers. The photo wasn't very clear, so when it was taken the dress could have been in shadow or in the light. And the lighting may have been natural daylight (which is blueish) or from an electric light (which is yellowish). That's important, because our brain depends on the light to decide what colour things really are.

A group of researchers set up an online study to find out more. The study went well, as 8,000 people responded and the results were interesting. There was a big difference between 'larks', who get up early and spend a lot of time in daylight, and 'owls', who stay up late and are more used to artificial light. Larks usually saw the dress as white and gold and owls usually saw it as blue and black.

However, the researchers say that there might have been other reasons for the difference. The study showed that it wasn't important where people lived or what time of day they viewed the photo. But the size of their screen made a difference – people who saw the dress on a bigger screen were more likely to see it as white and gold. Also, women were a bit more likely than men to see it as white and gold. It seems there's still a lot to learn about how we see colours!

One thing is certain. As a result of all this attention on social media, sales of the dress went up dramatically. The retailer produced the dress in white and gold as well as blue and black and they must have made a lot of money!

GRAMMAR
Modals of deduction (past)

4 Match 1–3 with a–c. Check your answers in the article on page 88. Then match sentences 1–3 with the rules.

1 You can't have
2 The dress could have
3 The retailer must have

a made a lot of money!
b been in shadow or in the light.
c missed it!

RULE:
To say something was possibly the case in the past, we use *might / could / may + have* + past participle. ☐
To say something was definitely not the case in the past, we use *couldn't / can't + have* + past participle. ☐
To say something was definitely the case in the past, we use *must + have* + past participle. ☐

5 Complete the conversation. Use suitable modals and the correct forms of the verbs in brackets.

'The Case of the Missing Cake'

Oliver What?! My cake! It's gone!
Matt Really?
Oliver Yes, it was here an hour ago and now it isn't. Who's taken it?
Matt What about Dad? I heard him saying how hungry he was. In fact, I'm sure it [1]______________ (be) Dad.
Oliver No, he [2]______________ (eat) it. It was chocolate. Dad doesn't like chocolate.
Matt That's true. I suppose Mum [3]______________ (take) it, maybe?
Oliver No, it [4]______________ (be) Mum. She's been out all morning.
Matt The dog! He [5]______________ (jump) onto the table and eaten it. That dog's always doing things like that.
Oliver Are you mad? The cake was in the fridge. The dog [6]______________ (got) to it.
Matt Are you sure it wasn't you? I mean, you [7]______________ (eat) it and forgotten.
Oliver I'm quite sure it wasn't me. So if it wasn't me, Mum, Dad or the dog, that leaves one person. It [8]______________ (be) you, Matt!
Matt What?! Me?
Oliver Yes, and that explains why you've got chocolate all round your mouth!

→ workbook page 83

FUNCTIONS
Making deductions

6 Read the text and complete the sentences with your opinions. Use *can't*, *must* or *might*.

In 1998, Russian scientists found a meteorite with a metal screw in it. The rock is at least 300 million years old. At that time, there weren't even any dinosaurs on the planet.

1 It ______ be fake.
2 There ______ have been intelligent life on Earth 300 million years ago.
3 I think someone ______ have made it as a joke.
4 It ______ be from another planet.
5 The scientists ______ have lied about it.

7 SPEAKING Work in pairs. Discuss your ideas.

VOCABULARY
Expressions with *go*

8 Find expressions 1–8 in the text on page 88. Match them with the definitions.

1 go for
2 go one step further
3 go viral
4 go well
5 go crazy
6 go up
7 go without saying
8 go on

a do something extra
b be satisfactory
c become very excited about something
d be obvious
e be shared by many people on the internet
f continue
g choose
h increase

9 Complete the sentences with the correct forms of the expressions in Exercise 8.

1 The party's ______________, I think. Everyone's having fun.
2 It ______________ that your mum and I will support you in your decision!
3 The football fans ______________ when their team won the match.
4 I ______________ the red one. It's cool.
5 He posted the photo and within days it ______________!
6 I drew a picture of my dream house. My brother ______________ and built it.
7 The price of bread has continued to ______________.
8 It was raining but we still ______________ playing. We didn't stop.

→ workbook page 84

Fiction

1 **Look at the picture. Make some predictions.**

- What do you think will happen to spoil this beautiful scene?
- What will happen to the woman in the red dress?
- Why will the flower seller get angry?

2 9.06 **Read and listen to the extract. Were your predictions correct?**

Wild Country by Margaret Johnson

Chapter 1 *The flower market mistake*

The woman in the red dress was holding some large yellow flowers to her face. Behind her, there were lots more flowers – big flowers, small flowers, flowers of every possible colour. I was very pleased I'd got up early to see Nice's famous flower market. It was beautiful, and it helped me to forget that I wasn't going to have a nice day. Or a nice ten days. Grant Cooper! Grant Cooper! I couldn't believe I was going to work with that man for ten days. It was going to be horrible. But I wouldn't think about it until I had to. And here, in the market, I could almost forget. There was colour all around me – not just the flowers, but also the people buying them in their summer clothes. Even the buildings behind the market were colourful – red and orange with blue windows. What a lovely picture it would make, if I only had my paints with me. But I did have a pencil somewhere. I could do a quick drawing. I still had a few minutes before I had to leave for the airport. I found the pencil in the bottom of my shoulder bag, together with an old letter. Soon my pencil was moving quickly over the back of the letter as I began to draw the woman in the red dress. She was smelling some red flowers now, and her hair was very blonde in the sunshine. As I drew what I saw, I quickly forgot about everything else. The woman buying the flowers obviously knew the flower seller. They were talking and laughing together, and I had lots of time to work on my picture.

I don't know how long I stood there. I only know that the next time I looked at my watch, it was nine o'clock. Nine o'clock! I only had thirty minutes to get to the airport. Oh no, I was going to be late. Again. But before I could put the pencil and paper back into my bag, I felt something soft against my legs. It was a small brown dog, and he was on his own. 'Hello, boy,' I said. 'Are you lost?' The dog seemed to smile up at me, and I reached out to touch it. The dog smiled again, and then … it bit me! I screamed and jumped quickly back from the dog. Too quickly. There was a very loud crash behind me. 'Mademoiselle!' shouted an angry voice. I turned round to see flowers all over the ground. 'I'm sorry,' I said. 'That dog – it bit me!' 'What dog?' asked the angry flower seller. 'Well, that one,' I said, but when I looked down, the dog had disappeared. 'It was here a minute ago,' I said, turning to look. Unfortunately, I turned so quickly that my shoulder bag flew through the air and crashed into some more flowers. 'Mademoiselle!' shouted the flower seller again. 'I'm sorry,' I started to say, but then I noticed that things were about to get even worse. A river of dirty water from the flowers was moving very quickly towards the blonde woman's expensive white summer shoes. 'Madame!' I shouted, but it was too late. 'My shoes!' cried the blonde woman. 'My flowers!' cried the flower seller. I held my hand up to show what the dog had done. 'My finger!' I cried, but neither the flower seller nor the blonde woman was interested in my hurt finger.

3 9.06 **Read and listen to the extract again. Answer the questions.**

1 What did the flowers help the woman to forget?
2 What did she draw the picture on?
3 Why did she stop drawing?
4 Why did the woman jump backwards?
5 How did she knock over the second lot of flowers?
6 Why was the blonde woman upset?

4 SPEAKING **Work in pairs. Discuss these questions.**

1 Has the woman really been bitten?
2 Will she find out more about the dog?
3 What will she find out?

WRITING
Explaining a mystery

1 INPUT **Read the article opposite. Who does the writer think is responsible for the crop circles?**

2 **Write the underlined expressions in the correct columns.**

I'm sure	I'm reasonably sure	I'm not sure

3 ANALYSE **The article has three paragraphs. What does the writer talk about in each one?**

4 PLAN **Read about a mystery. Then write three sentences about it. Use a different expression from Exercise 2 in each sentence.**

MISSING
HELICOPTER

An army helicopter with a pilot, co-pilot and twelve soldiers on board has disappeared off the north coast of Scotland. The last contact with the helicopter was more than 12 hours ago, when the pilot radioed that everything was OK. No distress signal was received and, despite a huge search over sea and land, no sign of the helicopter has been found. What has happened to army helicopter 487?

5 PRODUCE **Write a blog entry (200 words) explaining what you think happened to the missing helicopter.**

Mysterious patterns
appear in local field overnight

1 This isn't the first time such a thing has happened and it probably won't be the last time either. For decades, crop circles have been fooling experts, who are still asking, 'What exactly causes these patterns?'

2 Some people say aliens might create this phenomenon. They suggest that aliens come to Earth at night and leave these patterns in our fields. These people are definitely wrong. Even if aliens from other planets existed, how could they land a huge spaceship without anyone noticing? It would be impossible, of course.

3 Humans must have made these crop circles, just as they must have made all the others, but I'm not certain how they did it. Obviously, it can't have been done by just one person; it must have been a group and, more than likely, quite a large one. Also, it's clear that the person, or people, behind the design must be extremely intelligent because these patterns are extraordinarily complex. It was most probably organised by a group of Maths students from a university. It's the kind of thing that students like to do as a joke. But whoever did it, they've certainly got people talking.

10 MONEY

OBJECTIVES

FUNCTIONS: talking about future events; sympathising

GRAMMAR: future continuous; future perfect

VOCABULARY: money and value; jobs and work; *by*

Get THINKING

Watch the video and think: do you think it would be possible to live without money?

READING

1 **Look at the photos and answer the questions.**

1 Which of the payment methods do you recognise? Where are they used?
2 Which of them do you or your family use?

2 10.01 **Read and listen to the article. Mark the sentences T (true) or F (false) according to the article.**

1 Paper money was invented because of the weight of coins. ☐
2 In Sweden, cash is disappearing. ☐
3 Supermarkets will never use invisible payments. ☐
4 It's good to have computers looking after money systems, because they are 100% reliable. ☐
5 Security measures aren't a concern when thinking about privacy issues. ☐
6 In the future there might be payment systems we haven't thought of yet. ☐

Train to THINK

Exaggeration

Sometimes writers exaggerate to create dramatic effect. Of course, this doesn't mean that what they're saying is completely true.

3 **Look at these sentences from the article. Which words show that they're exaggerations?**

1 The answer is undeniably no.
2 By far, that's the most important question.

4 **Read the sentences. Which *isn't* an exaggeration? Write the words that help you decide.**

1 There's no way that credit cards will exist in ten years.
2 I found this subject really quite interesting.
3 It's the best article that has ever been written.

5 **Rewrite these sentences so they contain an exaggeration.**

1 It was a really boring film.
2 Justin Timberlake is a great singer.
3 Brian's good at Maths.

MONEY: PAST, PRESENT AND FUTURE

Thousands of years ago, people started using metal coins as money to buy and sell things. But the coins were heavy, so paper money was invented. Different payment systems evolved through time and now we also use credit and debit cards. These cards often have to be put into a machine and then a PIN has to be tapped in – but that practice is disappearing with contactless cards and smartphone apps becoming more and more popular. So, cash has mostly been replaced by alternative payment methods. And things don't stop there: it's possible that some countries will soon be completely cashless. For example, it's predicted that no one in Sweden will be using cash at all by about 2025.

So, what is the future of money? Twenty years from now, will we still be using cash? The answer is undeniably no. And it's highly likely that bank cards are on their way out as well. This is happening already: the use of smartphones, smartwatches and electronic wristbands has allowed people, in many situations, to avoid using cash or cards. Some apps let us transfer money from phone to phone like a text message, which makes it a quick and easy way to repay a friend if you owe them money. Increasingly, people are making 'invisible' payments for things like car rides – you choose a car, you take the ride, the money automatically comes out of your registered card. You can even include a tip for your driver this way! Perhaps we will soon be doing this in places like supermarkets, too – you'll get your goods, a reader will record the details of what you've bought as you leave and the amount will be taken automatically from your account. And if you need a refund, the money is put back in your account as easily as it was taken out.

Worry-free shopping. No machines or long check-out queues. No more heavy wallets or purses. This all sounds very positive, but there are possible disadvantages, too. Technological advancement, as we all know, brings many positives but also forces us to consider other matters. Will fraud, especially online, get easier? And as our money systems become more dependent on computers, how can we make sure that the computers don't fail? Security might get better as we increase our use of things like fingerprint and face identification, but will they be used to invade our privacy by gathering information about our movements? By far, that's the most important question.

Questions like these won't go away easily. We are in a state of change, and there are many different future possibilities. Perhaps unimagined payment methods will be developed. It will be interesting to see how things move forward, but one thing is for sure – in 20 years' time, we won't be buying, selling and paying the same way that we do now.

SPEAKING

6 **Work in pairs. Discuss these questions.**

1 Do you think a cashless society would be a good idea? Why or why not?

2 Do you think there will still be coins and banknotes in 30 years' time? Why or why not?

Grammar rap!

GRAMMAR
Future continuous

1 Complete the sentences from the article on page 93. Then choose the correct words to complete the rule.

1 Twenty years from now, will ____________ still ____________ cash?
2 Perhaps we ____________ soon ____________ this in places like supermarkets, too.
3 In 20 years' time, we ____________ buying, selling and paying the same way that we do now.

RULE: We use **the future continuous** to talk about things that will be in progress at [4]***a specified / an unspecified*** time in the future.

2 Complete the sentences with the correct forms of the verbs.

1 Tomorrow at 10 o'clock, I ____________ (sit) on a train.
2 Lucky you! This time next week, you ____________ (enjoy) your holidays.
3 Susan is still at university, but a year from now, she ____________ (work) in her dad's company.
4 What ____________ I ____________ (do) three years from now? I have no idea.
5 Talk to Sam now. Tonight he ____________ (play) tennis, so you won't be able to reach him.
6 Tomorrow afternoon, we ____________ (have) a coffee in a café next to the river.

3 Complete the text. Use the future simple or future continuous form of the verbs.

not travel | drink | wake up | put on
not work | pay | lie | have

I know where I'll be ten years from now. I [1]____________________ 50 hours a week in a small office. I [2]____________________ two hours every day to get to and from work. No, I [3]____________________ on a beautiful Caribbean beach! I [4]____________________ coconut water and reading a good book. Every day will be the same. I [5]____________________ late and I [6]____________________ a long, lazy breakfast. Every morning I [7]____________________ my shorts and walk down to the beach to meet my friends. And how [8]____________________ I ____________________ for all of this? That's an excellent question!

4 SPEAKING Work in pairs. Discuss what you will be doing at these times.

1 an hour from now
2 at 8 o'clock tonight
3 this time next week
4 on 1 January

An hour from now, I'll be having lunch.

→ workbook page 90

VOCABULARY
Money and value

5 Match the words with the definitions.

a tip | £(X) off | a reward | a bargain
owe | a refund | be worth
not good value for money | valuable | on offer

1 money that you get for doing something helpful (for example, finding something that was lost)
2 money that's paid back to you (for example, if you return something to a shop)
3 extra money to thank someone (for example, a waiter) for a service
4 to need to pay someone
5 available at a good price (usually for a short time)
6 money taken away from the original price
7 something you get at a really good price
8 not worth its price
9 having a very high value
10 to have a value of

6 Complete the sentences with the words from Exercise 5.

0 I'm not buying the shoes in this shop. There's another one nearby where they're *on offer* .
1 I ______ Kylie £20. I mustn't forget to repay her.
2 Mr Brown offered a big ______ for any information that would help him to find his cat.
3 The taxi driver was very helpful, so we gave him a good ______ .
4 Have a look at this old coin. Do you think it's ______ much?
5 I bought this expensive laptop last week. Today I saw it in the shop for £100 ______ .
6 The tablet didn't work, so I took it back to the shop and they gave me a ______ .
7 I paid £50 for this toy and it broke after a week. It really was ______ .
8 I waited until after the bank holiday and got the bike for half price. It was a real ______ .
9 This vase is 3,000 years old and very ______ .

7 SPEAKING **Work in pairs. Discuss the questions.**

1 What's the most valuable thing that teenagers usually own?
2 What are some good ways to get a bargain?
3 In what situations might you give someone a reward or a tip? Have you ever received one?
4 Have you ever had to ask for a refund? What for?

→ workbook page 92

LISTENING

8 **Look at the questionnaire and try to guess the answers. Then compare with a partner.**

9 10.02 **Listen to an extract from the quiz show *Moneyspinners*. Check your answers.**

WordWise: Phrases with *by*

10 **What do the phrases in bold refer to? Match 1–4 with a–d.**

1 Cash has mostly been replaced **by alternative payment methods**. ☐
2 She won £1,000 **by answering** questions about money. ☐
3 You can get money from the cash machine **by the entrance** to the supermarket. ☐
4 No one in Sweden will be using cash at all **by 2025**. ☐

a a location
b a time in the future
c a way to do something
d the person / people / thing(s) that do something

11 **Complete the sentences with the phrases.**

by the bus station | by the end of class
by the French teacher | by washing

1 Please finish Exercise 2 ________________ .
2 I was made to stay after class ________________ .
3 Meet me tomorrow ________________ downtown.
4 I made some money ________________ people's cars.

→ workbook page 92

PRONUNCIATION
Short and long vowel sounds: /ɪ/ – /iː/ and /ɒ/ – /əʊ/ Go to page 121.

ODD FACTS ABOUT MONEY

1 Some coins in … have holes in the middle.
A Britain
B Iceland
C Japan
D South Africa

2 More people take money from a cash machine (ATM) on … than any other day.
A Mondays
B Thursdays
C Fridays
D Saturdays

3 Of all the money in the world, only … is actual cash (coins and notes).
A 8%
B 12%
C 20%
D 50%

4 The first country to make plastic banknotes was …
A Sweden.
B Germany.
C the US.
D Australia.

5 The world's first known coin is called the …
A Egyptian Lira.
B Lydian Lion.
C Ying Yuan.
D Saxon Shilling.

READING

1 **Look at the people in the photographs. If Margaret Phelps earns £65,000 a year, how much do you think the other two get?**

Margaret Phelps: doctor

Andy Gardner: delivery man

2 **Read the article and posts quickly. Choose a suitable title.**

A Inequality isn't only about money
B A new kind of inequality
C Equality is impossible
D Continued inequality

3 10.05 **Read and listen to the article and posts. Which writer thinks:**

1 it's not always ability that determines who gets rich and who doesn't?
2 people can get good jobs because of who they know?
3 high salaries are OK because earners contribute to society?
4 differences in salaries are just part of life?
5 healthcare managers shouldn't earn more than medical professionals?
6 it's possible to earn a lot of money before you're very old?

Graham Hargreaves: company director

MONEYMATTERS HOME BLOG LOGIN

____

It's said that the easiest way to be really rich is to be born into a really rich family. That aside, undoubtedly the best way to become truly wealthy is to get a good idea for a product, make it and sell it, then sit back and watch the money come in. Throughout history, many people have become incredibly wealthy that way.

There's nothing new in this – for centuries people have had ideas, made things and become very rich. But questions are increasingly being asked about the way we're going. How fair is it for one person to have a personal fortune of billions of dollars? Is it right for big company bosses to be paid huge salaries and often to receive large bonuses on top of that? (In just one year, the head of a building company in the UK received £75 million in bonuses: is that acceptable?) In 1978, bosses in the UK's biggest companies earned on average about 30 times an ordinary employee's salary – in 1988 it was 47 times, but by 2020, this had increased to 133 times.

We'd like to hear your comments on this subject. 5 20 9

A I left school with a guy I know and we went to work in a finance company. His father's one of the directors, so now he's got a very well-paid job, earning five times as much as me. By the time he's 30, he'll have earned millions – and he does everything he can not to pay tax. It's sickening.

GBarker95

B I'm not sure what the problem is. It's just how the world is. Like the article says, there's nothing new here. Some people get lucky, some don't. Look at writers – lots of people get an idea and write a book, or books – and sometimes thousands of people buy the book and the writer gets rich. They're not even always the best writers. That's just how it is.

Thatcherman

C One time, I heard a politician say 'It's fine for people to be extremely rich – as long as they pay their taxes.' I agree. A top boss, after ten years of work or so, will have given millions of pounds back in taxes to help the country. And that benefits everyone, right?

Arguer123

D My mum's a doctor and she'll be working until she's 60 – 35 years of work – and when she stops, she won't have made a tenth of what some of these people make in a year. And there are people who manage the hospitals she works in who earn five times what she does. Who contributes more to healthcare – a doctor or someone who works in management? It's disgraceful.

Aliboy

GRAMMAR
Future perfect

4 Complete the sentences from the comments on page 96. Then read the rule and complete it with the words in the list.

1 A top boss, after ten years of work or so, ____________________ millions of pounds back in taxes.

2 When she stops, she ____________________ a tenth of what some of these people make in a year.

have | past participle | *will*

RULE: We use the future perfect to talk about actions that will finish at some time between now and a specified time in the future.

By the end of the year, he'll have made more than £3 million.

- We form it with [3] ______ + [4] ______ + [5] ______ .
- We often use it with *by* + a point in time or *by the time* + a time clause.
  By 2050, …
  By the time I'm 50, …

5 Complete the sentences with the future perfect form of the verbs.

1 The government ____________________ (build) lots of new houses here by 2030.

2 By the time I'm 35, I ____________________ (work) in IT for over ten years.

3 If I work really hard, I ____________________ (do) my homework by the time the match starts on TV.

4 The test is from 9 to 12 tomorrow morning. So at 10 o'clock, I ____________________ (not finish) it.

5 By that time, I ____________________ (buy) my first house.

6 I hope that three years from now, I ____________________ (visit) one or two other countries.

6 SPEAKING **Work in pairs. Look at the questions and make notes. Then compare your ideas.**

1 Which tasks will / won't you have finished by 6 pm tomorrow?

2 What will / won't you have done by the end of the year?

3 Which goals will you have achieved six years from now?

→ workbook page 90

VOCABULARY
Jobs and work

7 Match the words with the definitions.

education | employee | employer | finance | healthcare | law | management | public service | qualifications | salary

1 abilities or experience needed for a particular job
2 jobs paid for by the government
3 people who make the big decisions in a company
4 teaching and learning
5 a person or organisation that people work for
6 an area of work related to managing money
7 the money a person is paid for doing a job
8 an area of work related to the legal system
9 an area of work related to medicine
10 someone who's paid to work for someone else

8 Complete the sentences with words from Exercise 7.

1 Her dad works in ______ . He's a nurse.
2 Margaret Bourne is the director of ______ for a big company. She decides on all the investments.
3 Joanna was a police officer and now she's a teacher. She's been in ______ all her professional life.
4 Larry is a teacher. He works in ______ .
5 The company suffered years of bad ______ .
6 This tech company is the biggest ______ in the Seattle area.
7 A degree and some experience in IT are necessary ______ for this job.
8 James works in the ______ . He's a judge.
9 Allan got a new job with a higher ______ .
10 She's been an ______ of this company for 25 years.

9 SPEAKING **Work in pairs. Discuss these questions.**

1 Which of the areas of work in Exercise 7 would you be most / least interested in? Why?
2 Would you rather be an employer or an employee? Why?

→ workbook page 92

WRITING
My life in the future

10 Write about your life 30 years from now (150–200 words). Think about the things that you:

- will be doing.
- won't have done.
- will have done.
- will still want to do.

DEVELOPING SPEAKING

1 🔊 10.06 **Look at the photo. Where are the three people? What do you think they're talking about? Read and listen to check.**

Josh: That was a great cake. I wish I could buy another one – but I'm really strapped for cash, same as usual.

Tanya: Don't look at me. Sorry, but I've only got enough for my ice cream. Last week, I had to fix my bike. So I'm broke.

Josh: What a pity. Never mind, though, you'll get some pocket money soon, won't you?

Tanya: I hate not having money to do the things I want. My grandparents have spent their whole lives like that. Not me. I'm determined to be seriously rich when I'm older.

Josh: Your grandparents seem really happy to me. Maybe they never worried about material things.

Tanya: So I'm wrong to want to be rich?

Josh: No, I'm saying not everyone wants to be, that's all. You can be happy without a lot of money.

Tanya: I'm just ambitious. It's not my fault.

Mark: Hi, guys! All right?

Josh: Not bad, Mark. We're talking about money – or rather, not having it. We're both broke, basically.

Mark: That's a shame. But good news. I've had some luck. I sold my tablet online for £50. The food and drink are on me! What do you guys want?

Tanya: An ice cream please – and another cake for Josh?

Josh: No, I'm fine thanks. You should keep your money.

Mark: No, money's for spending as far as I'm concerned. OK, then: one ice cream for Tanya and two for me!

2 🔊 10.06 **Listen and read the dialogue again. Answer the questions.**

1 Why hasn't Tanya got any money?
2 Why doesn't she want to be like her grandparents?
3 How much did Mark sell his tablet for?
4 Who is going to buy food and drinks?

3 SPEAKING **Discuss the statements in pairs. Which do you agree with (if any)?**

1 I'm determined to be seriously rich when I'm older.
2 You can be happy without a lot of money.
3 Money's for spending as far as I'm concerned.

Phrases for fluency

4 **Find the underlined expressions in the dialogue. How do you say them in your language? Use the expressions to complete the dialogues.**

1 A I haven't got enough money for lunch.
B Well, ______________________ ! I can't pay because ______________________ – again!
C It's OK. I'll pay for the food. Lunch and drinks ______________________ !

2 A Hi, Jack How are you?
B Oh, ______________________ , really. Nothing changes a lot, does it?

3 A Wow, this room is really untidy!
B Hey! ______________________ ! Julie made the mess, not me.
C OK, calm down. I didn't say it was you. I just said it was untidy, ______________________ .

FUNCTIONS
Sympathising

KEY LANGUAGE
I'm really sorry (to hear that).
That's a shame.
How awful.
What a pity.
Never mind.

5 **Look back at the dialogue. Complete the extracts with some phrases from the Key Language box.**

Tanya So, I'm broke.
Josh 1 ______________________ !
2 ______________________ though, you'll get some pocket money soon.
Josh We're both broke, basically.
Mark 3 ______________________ !

6 SPEAKING **Work in pairs. Write two-line conversations like the one in Exercise 5 about each of these situations. Then act them out.**

You tell your friend that …
- your exam results are very bad.
- you lost some money.
- you broke your smartphone.

LIFE COMPETENCIES

Being determined is a positive quality to have and it's good to want to achieve things in life.

1 ▷ 27 **Watch the vlog. Match these people with the roles they play in Serena's dream of learning the guitar?**

1 her dad	a her mentor
2 her music teacher	b her motivation
3 her friends	c her inspiration

2 ▷ 27 **Watch the vlog again and answer the questions.**

1 How is she going to find the time to learn the guitar?
2 How did her dad inspire her?
3 What advice did her teacher give her?
4 What is she going to do with her friends?

3 Read the text. What is Harry's goal?

Last year, my aunty got ill with cancer. She has spent a year having treatment and she's recovering now, but I felt that I wanted to do something for her and other people who are ill. So, in two months' time I am doing a half marathon to raise money for a cancer charity. I'm not very good at running and during the first month of training, I hurt my ankle. My training also started in January when it was cold and often dark. It's been tough sometimes, but I'm so grateful to my mum, who encouraged me and ran with me on the cold mornings. So far I've raised £400, and I'm hoping to raise £500. My aunty is really proud of me, so I'm determined to finish for her. ***Harry***

4 Answer the questions about the text.

1 What difficulties has Harry had to overcome to try and achieve his goal?
2 What kind of special motivation does he have for being determined?
3 How much money has he raised?
4 How are other people helping him to achieve his goal?

Me and my world

5 Think of a time you were determined to do something and make notes.

- What did you want to do?
- Why did you want to do it?
- Were you successful?
- How did the experience make you feel?

6 Talk to your friend about the experience.

TIPS FOR BEING DETERMINED

- **Try not to get discouraged – don't give up if things don't work out for you at first.**
- **Being determined isn't the only thing that counts. Remember to think about how your actions might affect the people around you.**
- **It's OK to accept help even when you were determined to complete a task alone.**

TOWARDS B2 First for Schools

LISTENING
Sentence completion

→ workbook page 89

1 🔊 10.07 **You will hear Conner talking about the Royal Mint, where coins are made. For questions 1–10, complete the sentences with a word or short phrase.**

Someone who collects 1 ______________________ is known as a numismatist.
The Royal Mint is the 2 ______________________ mint in the world.
The Mint doesn't make 3 ______________________ ; that's the responsibility of the Bank of England.
When the Mint started, 4 ______________________ ruled England.
Work at the Royal Mint never 5 ______________________ .
In one 6 ______________________ , the Mint can produce 90 million coins.
The Mint produces coins for 7 ______________________ different nations as well as the UK.
A metal disc with nothing printed on it is called a 8 ______________________ .
In 2012, the Mint made coins to commemorate the 9 ______________________ and the Queen's Diamond Jubilee.
Because of security concerns, you can't 10 ______________________ the Royal Mint.

WRITING
Essay

→ workbook page 97

2 **In your English class, you have been talking about money. Now your English teacher has asked you to write an essay for homework.**

Write your essay using all the notes and giving reasons for your point of view. Give your opinion (for or against) in the last paragraph.

Is it more important to enjoy your job or to earn a lot of money?

Notes – write about:
1 material possessions
2 happiness and job satisfaction
3 ______________________ (your own idea).

Write your essay in 140–190 words.

VOCABULARY

1 Complete the sentences with the words / phrases in the list. There are four extra words / phrases.

unexplained | went on | bargain | mysterious | worth | employer | on offer
employee | alien | refund | go very well | owe | going for | salary

1 He's worked for that company for 25 years now. He's their oldest ______________ .
2 Nobody knows what happened to him. The mystery of his disappearance is still ______________ .
3 The rain was terrible, but the race ______________ despite it.
4 Michael lent me some money last month. I still ______________ him 75p.
5 I bought this camera for half price. It was a real ______________ !
6 You've paid too much for it. It isn't ______________ that much money.
7 I'm afraid the exam didn't ______________ . I'm sure I've failed it.
8 He's been training all year. He's ______________ a gold medal.
9 You know those trainers you like? They're ______________ at the moment! You should buy them.
10 It's broken. I think you should take it back and ask for a ______________ .

/10

GRAMMAR

2 Complete the sentences with the verbs in the list. There are two extra verbs.

might | should have | won't be working | must have | might have
will be living | will have written | couldn't have

1 She hurt her head when she fell off her scooter. She ______________ worn a helmet.
2 She's a really good runner. If she'd entered the race, she ______________ won it.
3 By the time I'm 25, I ______________ on a Greek island!
4 In ten years' time, I ______________ for anybody. I'll have my own company.
5 He got there too late. He ______________ prevented the accident.
6 By the time I'm 30, I ______________ my first novel.

3 Find and correct the mistake in each sentence.

1 He shouldn't has left the window open. That's how the burglar got in.
2 She might like the film if she had come.
3 In ten years' time, I hope I will have working in London.
4 Where will you living in 20 years' time?
5 He must be finished his homework by now.
6 In five years' time, I will have climb Mount Everest.

/12

FUNCTIONAL LANGUAGE

4 Choose the correct words.

1 A No way! This piece of rock *can't* / *mustn't* be from another planet.
B I don't agree with you. I think it *can* / *might* be.
2 A I'm *many* / *really* sorry I can't come to the football match with you.
B Never *mind* / *know*. You can come with me next week.
3 A Hi, guys. What would you like to eat? The food's *on* / *with* me!
B Great! Same as *normal* / *usual*, please!
4 A It goes without *seeing* / *saying* that Peter can't come on Saturday. He's crashed his scooter.
B How *shameful* / *awful*!

/8

MY SCORE /30

22–30 | 10–21 | 0–9

11 EMERGENCY!

OBJECTIVES

FUNCTIONS: expressing purpose; emphasising

GRAMMAR: verbs followed by gerund or infinitive; *to / in order to / so as to; so* and *such*

VOCABULARY: danger and safety; adjectives with negative prefixes

Get THINKING

Watch the video and think: have you ever been in a dangerous situation? What happened?

A

B

C

READING

1 **Look at the photos. What is the same about all of them? What is different in each one?**

2 **Read the sentences. Which photo(s) might each one refer to?**

1. It took the rescuers a long time to bring the victim down. ☐
2. The victim was given first aid before going to hospital. ☐
3. The helicopter emergency services managed to pull the victim out of the sea. ☐
4. After the rescue operation, the victim was taken to hospital for treatment. ☐

3 **Make a list of people and things that can help in an emergency. Compare your ideas with others in the class.**

Things	People
ambulance	*police officer*

4 **Look at the photos on the next page and the title of the news report. What do you think it's about? Read the report quickly and check your ideas.**

5 11.01 **Read and listen to the report. Mark the sentences T (true) or F (false).**

1. The boys had just finished playing a football match. ☐
2. There is no complete map of the caves. ☐
3. You can get a guided tour of the beginning of the cave all year round. ☐
4. It was two days before the police knew where the boys were. ☐
5. The rescue quickly turned into an international mission. ☐
6. The boys had been missing for two weeks before contact was made with them. ☐
7. The divers knew they had to get the boys out quickly. ☐
8. The boys had to dive through the tunnels to get to safety. ☐

Miracle UNDERGROUND

It was 23 June, 2018. Twelve members of the Wild Boars football team and their coach stood in front of the entrance to the Tham Luang cave in Northern Thailand. The boys, aged between 11 and 16, had finished training for the day and they decided to explore the cave. They left their bikes outside and took their torches and some snacks inside with them. It would be more than two weeks before the group saw daylight again.

The Tham Luang cave stretches 10 km into the mountain with a network of chambers, narrow passages and tunnels. Parts of the cave have been explored, but much of it hasn't. Inside there is no phone signal, so contact with the outside world is impossible. The first kilometre is open to the public, but only until June. In the rainy season from July to November it becomes extremely dangerous because the whole system quickly fills with water. And in June 2018 the rain came early.

When the boys failed to come home that evening, their parents contacted the police. Finding the bikes outside the cave, the police soon realised where they were, but they also knew that rainwater had flooded the caves. The boys and their coach were trapped somewhere inside and were in great danger.

At 4 am the next morning, Thai divers tried to start searching the cave, but it was soon clear that they did not have the equipment or experience they needed. News of the emergency soon spread. Within days experts from countries all over the world had arrived at the cave as they hoped to help rescue the group.

For days an international team of divers searched deep into the caves but found no sign of the group. Then, at last, on the tenth day, two British divers arrived in a new chamber where they saw 13 figures sitting on a shelf of rock above the water. The boys and their coach were very thin and weak, but they were alive. The celebrations, though, were short. The divers knew the boys weren't out of danger yet and that the rescue would be extremely difficult. They had 13 young people with no diving experience to bring to safety through 4 km of dark narrow passages. Furthermore, heavy rain was predicted and water levels would soon be rising. If they weren't brought out soon, it would be impossible to save them.

A team of experts worked night and day to plan the rescue. Each boy, dressed in a wetsuit and with a supply of oxygen, was taken underwater by a diver through the flooded chambers. The divers were guided by ropes to avoid losing their way and they kept checking the air bubbles to make sure the boys were breathing. In other parts of the cave, the boys lay on plastic stretchers which were pushed with great difficulty through the narrow spaces.

It took three days to get everyone to safety and the last person was brought out just as the water levels in the cave started to rise quickly. It was a miracle – all 13 members of the Wild Boars had survived.

Train to TH!NK

Understanding cause and effect

There is a cause-and-effect relationship between two ideas only if we can show that one thing leads to another.

6 Match the causes (1–5) with the effects (a–e). Then check your answers in the article.

1 The boys didn't come home. ☐
2 The police found the boys' bikes. ☐
3 It had rained a lot overnight. ☐
4 News of the emergency spread. ☐
5 The boys had been missing for ten days. ☐

a Experts from all over the world arrived to help.
b Most people thought they were dead.
c The caves were flooded.
d They knew the boys were in the cave.
e The parents contacted the police.

7 Complete 1–3 with a cause or an effect.

1 The flooding became worse, so the divers …
2 … , so we decided to call the emergency services.
3 … Therefore, the victim was taken to hospital.

SPEAKING

8 Work in pairs. Discuss these questions.

1 Do you think the divers were heroes? Why or why not?
2 Do you know any stories of ordinary people being heroes?

GRAMMAR
Verbs followed by gerund or infinitive

1 **Complete the sentences from the news report on page 103. What do the verbs have in common?**

1 They decided ______ the caves.
2 The boys failed ______ home.
3 They hoped ______ rescue the group.

2 **Now complete these sentences from the report. What do these verbs have in common? Then complete the rule. Label the columns with *to + infinitive* or *gerund*.**

1 The boys, aged between 11 and 16, had finished ______ for the day.
2 The divers were guided by ropes to avoid ______ their way.
3 Divers kept ______ the air bubbles.

RULE:

Followed by [4] ______	Followed by [5] ______
avoid, enjoy, feel like, finish, imagine, keep, (don't) mind, miss, practise, (can't) stand, suggest	afford, choose, decide, expect, fail, hope, learn, offer, promise, want

3 **Complete the sentences. Use a verb from A followed by a verb from B in each sentence.**

A avoid | ~~choose~~ | decide | feel like | finish | hope
B buy | go | see | speak | ~~stay~~ | watch

0 I can't believe you ***chose to stay*** at home last night rather than come to the cinema with us.
1 After a lot of thought, I ______ a new bike.
2 Bye! I ______ you again soon.
3 I'm so tired. I just ______ to bed.
4 I really don't like him, so I ______ to him.
5 I'll help you. I'll just ______ this video first.

→ workbook page 100

PRONUNCIATION
Strong and weak forms: /tuː/ and /tə/
Go to page 121.

VOCABULARY
Danger and safety

4 **Replace the underlined phrases with the words and phrases in the list.**

rescued | dangerous | in danger | to safety | survived | recover | save his life | out of danger

1 He was in a terrible accident, but he didn't die.
2 Don't go into that room! There might be something that could hurt you in there.
3 She went to hospital to get better.
4 The firefighter took the baby away from a dangerous situation.
5 The doctors managed to prevent him from dying.
6 People who lived near the volcano moved away so they were not going to be harmed.
7 People who drive really fast sometimes put their lives in a situation where they are likely to be harmed.
8 The helicopter took him to a place where he wasn't going to be harmed.

5 **Choose the correct words.**

1 Thank you so much – you *rescued / saved* my life!
2 We can go in here. It isn't *safe / dangerous* at all.
3 We were lucky to *survive / save* the accident.
4 The boat sank, but all the passengers were *recovered / rescued* by another boat.
5 Fortunately, he *recovered / saved* from his injuries.
6 No one died. All the passengers *rescued / survived*.
7 She was badly hurt in the accident, but fortunately she's *in / out of* danger now.
8 The helicopter flew the survivors *in danger / to safety*.

6 SPEAKING **Work in pairs or small groups. Discuss these questions.**

1 In which sports and activities are people in danger? Do you do them? Would you like to? Why or why not?
2 Do you know of someone who has been in a bad accident and survived? How did he/she survive?
3 Do you know anyone who's saved another person's life? Who was it? What happened?

→ workbook page 102

LISTENING

7 In which picture can you see these things?

arena | emperor | gate | master
paw | slave | thorn

8 11.04 **You're going to hear a story called *Androcles and the Lion*. Put the pictures in the order you think tells the story. Then listen and check.**

9 11.04 **Listen again. Answer the questions.**

1 Why didn't Androcles run from the lion in the forest?
2 Why did his master want to execute Androcles?
3 Why didn't the lion attack Androcles?
4 What did the emperor do and why?
5 What does the presenter think the moral is?

10 SPEAKING **Work in pairs or small groups. What do you think the moral of the story is? Do you know any other stories with morals?**

11 SPEAKING **Mark these statements 1–5 (1 = I strongly agree; 5 = I strongly disagree). Then discuss your answers in small groups.**

1 Helping someone else makes me feel good. ☐
2 I only help someone when they ask me to. ☐
3 You can always help another person. ☐
4 I only help people when I think they can also help me. ☐
5 I try to do something myself before I ask for help. ☐

GRAMMAR

to / in order to / so as to

12 Look at the sentences from the listening. Then complete the rule.

1 Androcles managed to escape and went to the forest to hide.
2 Androcles took it in his hand so as to see what the problem was.
3 The lion was kept in a cage for days without food in order to make him as hungry as possible.

RULE: We can use ***to*** + infinitive to talk about purpose. In more formal language or in writing, we can also use [4]_______ or [5]_______ + infinitive.

13 Think about the stories in the unit so far. Match 1–4 with a–d. Then rewrite each pair as one sentence using the words in brackets.

0 Why did Androcles pull the thorn from the lion's paw? *e*
Androcles pulled the thorn from the lion's paw to help the lion.
1 Why did the divers use ropes? ☐
2 Why did the international divers go to Thailand? ☐
3 Why did the boys need oxygen? ☐
4 Why was the lion put into the arena? ☐

a help the boys breathe underwater. (to)
b kill Androcles. (in order to)
c avoid losing their way. (so as to)
d help save the boys. (in order to)
e ~~help the lion~~. (to)

→ workbook page 100

FUNCTIONS

Expressing purpose

14 Match 1–5 with a–e.

1 Why did she send you a card? ☐
2 Why did you get up early yesterday? ☐
3 Why did you go into town? ☐
4 Why did he save his money for so long? ☐
5 Why did they move house? ☐

a to watch the sun come up
b in order to get a new guitar
c so as to have more room
d to get a present for my mum
e to say thank you

15 SPEAKING **Work in pairs. Think of three *Why do / did you ...?* questions to ask your partner. Ask and answer each other's questions.**

READING

1 In the UK, you dial 999 for the emergency services. What number do you call in your country? Does it depend on the type of emergency?

2 11.05 Read and listen to the article. Which of the 'emergency' calls do pictures A–C show?

EMERGENCY? *What emergency?*

An emergency service should be exactly that: a service that you phone in an emergency. You might need to call an ambulance if you're in a car accident or the police if you see a crime happening. But some people phone the emergency services for such unimportant reasons that it's hard to believe these calls are real. Then again, there are some strange people out there, so perhaps it isn't really so surprising that the emergency services get some unusual calls.

1 One football fan was so angry that his team, Manchester United, had lost an extremely important match that he phoned the emergency services after the match and demanded to speak to the team's manager, Sir Alex Ferguson.

2 There was also a man who phoned the police after his son refused to get off his game console late at night. He said they'd had such a bad argument that he wanted them to come and put the boy to bed.

3 One woman couldn't find her glasses and thought the emergency services might help. She complained that she was trying to peel potatoes, but her eyesight was so bad that she couldn't see what she was doing.

4 Once, a man dialled 999 when he found that his snowman had gone missing. He had left his house for five hours to find that it had gone when he returned. He said he was really angry and wanted the police to check CCTV footage of the area.

5 The emergency services received a call from a woman to tell them that she had such a bad memory that she couldn't remember the password for her computer. She was so disappointed when they explained that they couldn't help her.

6 When one man's friend threw his shoes onto a supermarket roof as a joke, he phoned 999 and asked if the fire engine could come and help him get them down. He even offered to climb up to the roof himself if they could just bring a ladder.

7 One woman called up to complain that her husband was such a lazy man because he wouldn't bring her her dinner while she sat and watched TV.

8 Finally, one time a woman was so upset about a squirrel in her garden that didn't have any nuts that she phoned to say she wanted the emergency services to find someone to bring it some food. She was worried it would starve.

These calls are amusing to read about, but they can have very serious consequences. 'It's such a waste of time! Every call takes about a minute,' said one man who works in the call centre for the emergency services. 'Perhaps that doesn't sound a very long time, but in that one minute, other people are calling who really have an emergency. And for them, a minute might be extremely important.'

So let's get serious: please THINK before you call the emergency services. And, of course, remember that you should never phone them with information that's untrue – it's irresponsible and it's also illegal.

3 Read the first and last paragraphs again. Answer the questions.

1 What examples are given of real emergencies?
2 Why should you never phone emergency services with untrue information?

4 SPEAKING Work in small groups. Which of the calls do you think was the craziest?

GRAMMAR
so and *such*

5 Complete the sentences from the article on page 106. Then complete the rule.

1 She was ______ disappointed when they explained that they couldn't help her.
2 One woman called up to complain that her husband was ______ a lazy man.

> RULE: We can use ***so*** or ***such*** to emphasise adjectives, adverbs, nouns and noun phrases:
> [1]______ + adjective / adverb
> [2]______ (+ ***a*** / ***an***) (+ adjective) + noun

6 Now complete these sentences from the article and complete the rule.

1 She had ______ that she couldn't remember the password for her computer.
2 Her eyesight was ______ that she couldn't see what she was doing.
3 They'd had ______ that he wanted the police to come and put the boy to bed.
4 One man was ______ that his team, Manchester United, had lost an extremely important match that he phoned the emergency services.

> RULE: We also use ***so*** or ***such*** to show how one thing is a result of another. The clause with ***so*** or ***such*** is followed by ______ + a result clause.

7 Join the pairs of sentences. Use *so* / *such* … *that*.

0 We were very late. We had to take a taxi.
We were so late that we had to take a taxi.
1 It was a very bad accident. Two people had to go to hospital.
2 It was very windy. It was dangerous to walk there.
3 The music was very loud. I couldn't fall asleep.
4 The road was very icy. It was dangerous to drive on it.
5 They were careless people. They always forgot to lock the door to their house.

→ workbook page 101

VOCABULARY
Adjectives with negative prefixes

8 Replace the underlined words with one word.

0 The divers were not concerned about their own safety.
unconcerned
1 It was not possible to get the boys out together.
2 The Manchester United fan was not happy because his team had lost.
3 It's not surprising that the emergency services get so many crazy calls.
4 Some people call 999 for not important reasons.
5 These not necessary calls take up a lot of time.
6 You should never phone with information that's not true – it's not responsible and it's also not legal.

9 Which negative prefixes do these adjectives take? Write them in the correct columns.

afraid | comfortable | concerned
expensive | formal | healthy | helpful
legal | logical | patient | polite
possible | regular | responsible | ~~surprising~~

un–	im–	in–	ir–	il–
unsurprising				

10 Complete the questions. Use adjectives from Exercise 9 with negative prefixes.

0 Do you think it's very *impolite* to talk with food in your mouth?
1 Do you think it's ______ to eat fried food?
2 Do you worry about exams, or are you ______ ?
3 Do you sometimes get a little ______ when you have to wait for things?
4 Do your parents think you're too ______ to be at home alone all weekend?
5 Do you think that ______ clothes are always bad quality?

11 SPEAKING Work in pairs. Discuss the questions in Exercise 10.

→ workbook page 102

THINK

The Great Escape

Culture

1 Look at the photos. What type of survival stories do they suggest?

2 11.06 Read and listen to the article. Check your answers.

B

The Great ESCAPE

After many tragedies, there are always stories of people who have shown an amazing ability to survive. Here are two stories which remind us that miracles can happen.

On 5 August, 2010, the San José copper and gold mine in the Atacama Desert in Chile collapsed and 33 miners were trapped underground. The mine had a poor safety record and there were fears that the missing men wouldn't come out alive. A rescue team immediately began drilling into the ground where it was thought the men might be. On Day 17, when the drill was brought out of the ground, there was a note taped to it. In bright red letters it read: 'We are alive and well in the shelter, all 33 of us.' It was the news the whole country had been waiting for and the Chilean government promised to bring them out alive. For the next seven weeks, rescue teams from all over the world worked together to drill a hole big enough to bring out the men, who were waiting 700 metres below the ground. It was a long, difficult and dangerous job, but on 13 October, more than a billion people around the world watched live on TV as the first of the miners was finally brought above ground. Twenty-four hours later, the last miner, number 33, was reunited with his family and friends.

A

In June 2013, a rescue diver was swimming through the wreck of the tugboat *Jascon-4* when he got an enormous shock: a hand reached out and grabbed his leg. The ship had sunk two and a half days earlier and was now lying 30 metres below the surface of the water. The diver, who was part of a team looking for the bodies of the 13 crew members, hadn't expected to find anyone alive. But one man had managed to survive. Twenty-nine-year-old Harrison Okene from Nigeria was the ship's cook. When the ship got into trouble in rough seas and started turning over, Okene found an air pocket and put his head in it. As the ship sank towards the sea floor, he expected the pocket to fill with water, but it didn't. Despite the freezing water and having nothing to eat or drink, Okene had enough air to breathe. There was nothing he could do except wait. Sixty hours after the ship went down, Okene heard knocking and knew that rescue teams had entered the ship. He still wasn't safe, and a complicated plan was needed to bring him slowly to the surface. Unfortunately, none of the other crew members survived. But for one man, the tragedy had ended with a miracle.

3 Read the article again. What do these numbers refer to?

0 7 *The number of weeks the miners were trapped underground.*

1 13 2 17 3 29
4 30 5 33 6 60

4 SPEAKING Work in pairs. Discuss these questions.

1 What do you think these people did while they were waiting to be rescued?

2 These people had accidents at work. Do you think people should be rescued when they are doing dangerous things for pleasure, for example, climbing mountains? Why or why not?

5 VOCABULARY There are seven **highlighted** words or phrases in the article. Match the words with these meanings. Write the words.

1 a space where water doesn't get in
2 the history of accidents at a place
3 gone down in the water
4 a terrible event that often kills many people
5 amazing events that almost seems impossible
6 an instrument that makes a hole in the ground
7 what's left of a car, ship, plane, etc. after a crash

WRITING
A story about a rescue

1 INPUT **Read the story. Answer the questions.**

1 Why did the boy and his friends walk across open land?
2 How long did the rescue take?
3 Why did he need to go to hospital?
4 How did his mother feel about the rescue?

2 **Complete the story with the words.**

after | and | because | but
later | where | which

3 ANALYSE **The story has four paragraphs. Which of them:**

a gives details about how the accident happened? ☐
b gives people's reactions to the accident? ☐
c gives a summary of the whole event? ☐
d describes how the accident was dealt with? ☐

4 PRODUCE **Think of a rescue that you know about or invent one. Write your story (200 words). Think about:**

- who was involved in the accident and the rescue.
- any special words that you will need to talk about the accident. (Use a dictionary to help you.)
- how to organise the information into paragraphs.
- how to make the story dramatic.

1 In March 2014, 14-year-old Za'Quan Clyburn from North Carolina, USA, was rescued [1]_____ he got trapped in mud.

2 Za'Quan was walking home with some friends. To save time, they walked across some open land [2]_____ was being prepared for building. Za'Quan walked down a hill towards a large pool of water. He thought the ground was solid [3]_____ that he could walk across it, but it was mud. He sank into it and couldn't get out. The mud went up to his chest and then almost to his chin.

3 One of his friends called 911. Firefighters arrived and started to work to get Za'Quan out. It took 24 people about half an hour to free him. Za'Quan was extremely cold and in shock, and his legs were very painful [4]_____ of the pressure of the mud. An ambulance took him to hospital, [5]_____ he was kept for two days.

4 One of the firefighters said, 'The outcome could have been much worse, [6]_____ fortunately he came through it OK.' The boy's mother said [7]_____ that she was really grateful to the people who had worked so hard and risked their lives to save her son.

12 LIFE'S FIRSTS

OBJECTIVES

FUNCTIONS: expressing regret; talking about fears

GRAMMAR: phrasal verbs; *I wish* / *If only* + past perfect

VOCABULARY: phrasal verbs (2); nervousness and fear

Get THINKING

Watch the video and think:
what is your earliest memory? How old were you?

READING

1 SPEAKING **Look at the photos. Which of these first experiences do *you* remember? Tell your partner. What other things can you remember doing for the first time?**

I remember my first day at school. I was six and I cried.

I think I can remember the first time I ...

2 Read the blog posts on the next page quickly. Which posts recall stressful moments?

3 12.01 **Read the posts again and listen. Answer the questions.**

1. What did Emma find difficult at dinnertime?
2. What did Emma splash all over herself?
3. Why did Paul go to hospital?
4. Why couldn't he sleep well there?
5. What was the problem that Susie had during the play?
6. How did she get the other actor to come on stage?

Train to THINK

Logical conclusions

Pay attention to conclusions in a text. Look at the ideas and arguments carefully. Do they lead logically to the conclusion?

4 Here is a conclusion from one of the posts. Is it a logical conclusion? Why or why not?

It was really strange that she never wrote back, but I'm sure she never got my emails.

5 Look at the underlined conclusions. Which aren't logical? Why?

1. Some Bradley Cooper films are brilliant. He's in *Avengers: Endgame*. It must be a good film.
2. The chef of the restaurant around the corner is famous for his steak. Jane often eats there. Therefore, Jane often eats steak.
3. Apples are very healthy fruit. I often eat apples. I have a healthy diet.
4. Tina has fair skin and burns very easily. She's going to Brazil for a beach holiday. She needs to protect her skin from the sun.

THE FIRST TIME I ...

We asked readers to tell us some of their 'first times' and here are three that we liked.

My first time eating spaghetti – Italian style

My best friend in my first year at school was Italian. Her name was Caterina Ricci. We were very different, but we got on really well and went everywhere together. The first time I went to her house, we had spaghetti for dinner. I asked for a spoon, but when Caterina started giggling I knew I had made a mistake. Italians only eat pasta with a spoon when it's in a broth, she told me. No big deal – watching Caterina I tried to [1]work out how to eat pasta the Italian way. I tried to spiral it around my fork like she did, but all I managed was to splash the tomato sauce all over myself. I guess I finished ten minutes later than everyone else. Nobody said anything, but I must have looked great in my white shirt covered in tomato stains! Caterina and her parents [2]moved away soon afterwards. I wrote to her a couple of times, but she didn't reply. It was really strange that she never wrote back, but I'm sure she never got my emails.

Emma

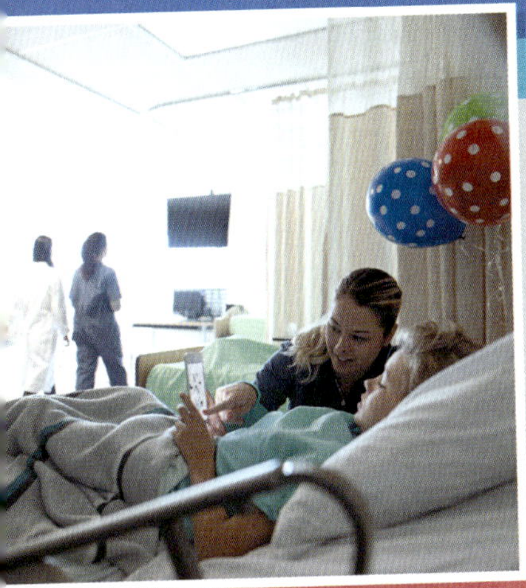

My first time in hospital

One winter day, I went ice-skating with some friends. I fell over, hit my head on the ice and knocked myself out. My friends were worried but I quickly [3]came round. When I told my mum and dad what had happened, they took me to the hospital. The doctor decided to keep me in overnight for some tests. There were other patients in the ward with me. One of them had had his wisdom teeth taken out. It was the first time I'd heard the words 'wisdom teeth' and it sounded strange to me. I remember that I tried to talk to him, but when he spoke I couldn't make out the words, so I couldn't understand what he was saying. I felt miserable, even though the nurses [4]looked after me and tried to [5]cheer me up. I didn't sleep well at all. It was my first night away from home and I've never forgotten it.

Paul

My first time on stage

I remember the excitement as everyone [6]put their make-up on and got into their costumes. I also remember how nervous I felt just before the curtain went up. I thought I wouldn't remember any of my lines. But in the end I didn't really have to worry about that. Everything started off well, but in the middle of the play I [7]ran into a problem. It was in a scene with the actor who played the role of my husband. He was supposed to come on stage, but I could see him offstage talking to someone. I knew he was going to miss his entrance. He didn't come on stage, so I had to [8]make some lines up and try not to panic! It seemed like hours, although it was probably only a few seconds. Then I said: 'I wonder where my husband is?' He heard me, came on stage and we carried on with the scene. I don't think the audience noticed anything wrong.

Susie

SPEAKING

6 Work in pairs or small groups. Discuss these questions.

1 How did the various people feel about their 'life first' experiences?
2 Would you have felt the same in their position?
3 What personal experiences did the stories remind you of?

VOCABULARY
Phrasal verbs (2)

1 Find the phrasal verbs in the blog posts on page 111. Match the verbs (1–8) with the definitions (a–h).

a place (clothing, make-up) on your body so as to wear it ☐
b go to live in a different town or place ☐
c become conscious again ☐
d invent, create ☐
e take care of ☐
f make someone feel happy ☐
g meet a person or a problem without expecting to ☐
h understand, find the answer to ☐

2 Complete the sentences with the correct forms of the phrasal verbs from Exercise 1.

0 It isn't a true story – I *made* it *up*.
1 He is often very sad. I find it difficult to ______ him ______ .
2 Yesterday, I ______ my best friend from primary school.
3 This question is really difficult. I can't ______ the answer.
4 We're going on holiday – can you ______ our cats while we're away, please?
5 When he fell, he became unconscious but, luckily, he ______ again after a minute.
6 I don't like this place any more. I think we should ______ .
7 If you haven't got a hat, please______ some sun lotion at least.

→ workbook page 110

GRAMMAR
Phrasal verbs

3 Look at these sentences from the text on page 111. In which ones does the object go between the two parts of the phrasal verb? Then complete the rule with the words.

1 I had to make some lines up.
2 The nurses looked after me.
3 They tried to cheer me up.

between (x2) | separated (x2) | together

RULE: With some phrasal verbs, the two parts can't be [4]______ . They have to be [5]______ .
*They **looked after** me.*
Other phrasal verbs can be [6]______ . We can put an object [7]______ the two parts or after the second part.
*I **put** my make up **on**.*
OR
*I **put on** my make up.*
When we use a pronoun (*him*, *it*, etc.) with a phrasal verb that can be separated, it must go [8]______ the two parts of the verb.
I worked it out.
I put it on.
How do you know if a phrasal verb can be separated?
Use a dictionary to look it up!
look sth up ➜ it can be separated
look into sth ➜ it can't be separated

4 Put the words in order to make sentences. When there are two possible orders, write both.

0 ago / moved / three / They / away / years
They moved away three years ago.
1 part / I'm / a / competition / in / taking
2 look / We / them / after / have to
3 excuse / made / an / She / up
4 joke / cheer / I / I / him / a / to / up / him / told
5 put / cold / It / she / jacket / was / so / her / on / that

5 SPEAKING Complete the questions with the correct forms of the phrasal verbs. Then discuss them in small groups.

look after | work out | move away
put on | run into | cheer up

1 When do you ______ smart clothes?
2 Have you ever ______ a friend in the street?
3 How do you ______ a friend if they're sad?
4 How do you ______ difficult problems?
5 Do you enjoy ______ animals or small children?
6 How would you feel if your best friend ______ ?

→ workbook page 108

LISTENING

6 SPEAKING **Work in pairs. Read the quiz questions. What do you think the answers are?**

QUIZ: TRANSPORT FIRSTS

1 Who built the first car?
A Karl Benz B Henry Ford C Gottlieb Daimler

2 Who was the first pilot to fly across the Channel from France to England?
A Amelia Earhart B Louis Blériot C Amy Johnson

3 Who was the first person to travel into space?
A Yuri Gagarin B Neil Armstrong C Valentina Tereshkova

4 The first hot air balloon to carry passengers, over 200 years ago … how far did it travel?
A 9 metres B 9 km C 19 km

5 Where was the first underground line built?
A Paris B Istanbul C London

7 12.02 **Listen to the same quiz on a radio show. Check your answers.**

8 12.02 **Listen again. Complete the notes.**

1 The first car
Where? ______________________
When? ______________________

2 First cross-Channel flight
Nationality of pilot? ______________________
When? ______________________

3 First person in space
Nationality? ______________________
When? ______________________

4 First hot air balloon flight
Where? ______________________
When? ______________________

5 Oldest underground line
Opened when? ______________________
Name of first line? ______________________

9 SPEAKING **Work in pairs. Answer the questions.**

1 Which of the 'transport firsts' do you think is the most important?
2 Do you think these 'transport firsts' will ever happen? If yes, when?

- [ ] passenger travel to the moon
- [ ] non-stop flights from New York City to Sydney, Australia
- [ ] trains that travel at 1,000 kph

TH!NK values

Breaking new ground

10 **Match the people (1–5) with their achievements (a–e).**

1 Neil Armstrong [ ]
2 Nelson Mandela [ ]
3 Charles Lindbergh [ ]
4 Kathryn Bigelow [ ]
5 Marie Curie [ ]

a was the first female director to win an Oscar.
b was the first man on the moon.
c was the first woman to win a Nobel Prize.
d was the first man to fly alone across the Atlantic.
e was the first black president of South Africa.

11 SPEAKING **Work in small groups. Discuss these questions.**

1 Is it important to be the first person to do something? Why or why not?
2 What's more important: coming first (for example, in a competition) or just taking part?

READING

1 From looking at these pictures, what do you think *arachnophobia* means?

2 SPEAKING Discuss in pairs or small groups how you or people you know react when seeing a spider?

3 12.03 Read and listen to the story. Mark the sentences T (true) or F (false).

1 Over ten percent of people in the US are afraid of spiders. ☐
2 Allen thinks spiders can harm him. ☐
3 Allen didn't play the game alone. ☐
4 When he saw 'Itsy' for the first time, he didn't want to continue the game. ☐
5 Allen expected that the game would not be fun. ☐
6 When Allen let the spider down, he didn't feel sorry at all. ☐
7 Allen thinks people with other fears won't find the app useful. ☐
8 Allen's sister went to the psychologist with him. ☐

4 Do you think Allen's sister will use the app, too? Why or why not?

THE FIRST TIME I MADE FRIENDS WITH A SPIDER

Allen was one of the 15 percent of teenagers in the US to have an extreme fear of something – also called a phobia. Allen's problem was arachnophobia: the fear of spiders. His phobia was so bad he couldn't be in a room with a spider. I asked him what he thought made spiders so terrifying. 'It's the quick movement, the dark colour, the legs,' he said. 'I couldn't look at them. I trembled if I saw one and I'd start to panic.' He knew that the spiders in his house weren't dangerous and couldn't hurt him, so there was no real reason to be scared of them, but he just couldn't control his reaction.

When Allen went to see a psychologist, she told him about the Virtual Reality app *Phobia Free*. He decided to give it a try.

Allen sat with the psychologist while he played the game. I asked him how it worked. 'I was asked to sit at a computer,' he told me. 'Then the psychologist told me I was going to meet a spider called Itsy. It felt a bit scary at first and I was glad the psychologist was with me. But when Itsy – a cartoon style animated spider – appeared, I couldn't help but smile. Itsy is fun and friendly and supports the person who has the phobia by making them kind of forget about the fear they want to overcome. And I must say I hadn't expected I would be playing an interactive game with a spider that would be so much fun! First, I was asked to help Itsy and its friends survive in difficult situations. For example, I had to help them avoid a vacuum cleaner. The game works like any computer game, but I soon noticed that I was developing an emotional link with the spiders. I really wanted to help them, and when I couldn't, I felt sorry for them!

If I do start to feel stressed or panicky, the app has relaxation and breathing exercises that really help to calm me down. They're not just for arachnophobes like me – people who have any kind of fear or phobia will find these exercises useful.

What's more, there's a real difference now in how I react to spiders in the real world. So, for the first time in my life, I recently touched a real spider. I saw it on my desk just in front of me. I kept really calm. I stretched out my hand, and let it run over it. Wow! It wasn't as much fun as playing with Itsy, my virtual friend, but I was amazed that I was OK with it. If only I'd tried this programme earlier! I might have avoided all that panic whenever I saw a spider. My sister has the same phobia and I wish she'd started this programme with me, but she said the thought of it was just too frightening. Now, though, she wants to try it.'

5 SPEAKING Work in pairs or small groups. Choose a different fear and design an app for it, with four or five different kinds of activities. What would they be like?

PRONUNCIATION
Different pronunciations of *ea* Go to page 121.

GRAMMAR
I wish / *If only* + past perfect

6 Complete the sentences from the text on page 114. Use the correct form of the verbs. Then complete the rule.

start | try

1 If only I ______ this programme earlier.
2 I wish she ______ this programme with me.

RULE: To express regret about the past, we can use *I wish* or *If* [3]______ + the [4]______ tense.

7 Write sentences with *I wish* … or *If only* … .

0 I didn't eat breakfast. Now I'm hungry.
I wish I'd eaten breakfast.
1 I didn't go to bed early. Now I'm tired.
2 I didn't ask her for her phone number.
3 Only 12 percent?! I didn't study last weekend.
4 Dad feels bad because he forgot Mum's birthday.
5 My friends are annoyed about missing the end of the film. They fell asleep!

8 Think of three things you've done recently that you now regret. Write sentences with *I wish* … and *If only* … .

family | friends | holidays
money | school | shopping

→ workbook page 109

FUNCTIONS
Expressing regret

9 Put the lines in order to make a conversation.

☐ **Oliver** I'm sorry to hear that.
☐ **Oliver** What's the matter, Amelia?
☐ **Oliver** Maybe you should lie down for a few minutes.
☐ **Amelia** It was that third piece of cake. I wish I hadn't eaten it.
☐ **Amelia** That isn't a bad idea. I think I will.
☐ **Amelia** I've eaten too much. I'm feeling ill.

10 SPEAKING Work in small groups. Discuss your regrets from Exercise 8 above. Make suggestions using expressions from the conversation in Exercise 9.

VOCABULARY
Nervousness and fear

11 Look at the words and phrases in bold in sentences 1–4. Match them with the pictures.

1 I was so **terrified** that I started **biting my nails**.
2 I was really **sweating**. In the end, I just **panicked** and ran out of the room.
3 When I saw the crowd in front of me, my mouth **went dry** and I started to breathe hard.
4 I started to **tremble**. In fact, I was **shaking** for about 15 minutes.

12 SPEAKING Work in pairs. What fears do the photos represent? What other things are some people afraid of?

13 Write sentences about your fears or those of people you know. Use words and phrases from Exercise 11. Then compare with a partner.

My uncle is afraid of heights. He starts to sweat, even if it's just in a film!

→ workbook page 110

Fiction

1 🔊 12.06 **Look at the picture. What kind of place is this? Read and listen to the introduction to check your ideas.**

Bullring Kid and Country Cowboy by Louise Clover

‘So are you looking forward to our holiday, Fizza?’ asked her dad.

‘No,’ thought Fizza.

‘Yes, she is!’ interrupted her mum. ‘Aren’t you, darling?’

Fizza smiled falsely […].

Fizza McIntyre is a city girl from Birmingham, UK. One year her parents hire a holiday cottage on the very small island of Sark, where there are no cars. Fizza goes along, to keep her parents happy. She doesn’t know that a big adventure is going to start.

2 🔊 12.07 **Read and listen to the rest of the extract. Complete the gaps with the missing time expressions (a–h) below.**

a Then, lifting her nose into the air
b Later, after supper
c By the time you get back
d As she began the climb back up the hill
e For over an hour
f In five minutes
g Eventually
h For a moment

And so it was that Fizza found herself on ‘the island that time forgot’ with absolutely nothing to do.

Her mum’s voice brought her out of her dream and back to the present moment.

‘Why don’t you go and explore, Fizza?’ said her mum. ‘[1]______________________, I’ll have supper ready. Oh! And get your dad a newspaper, please.’

Fizza went down the hill towards the little village at the bottom. [2]______________________ she had discovered two bicycle hire shops, three shops that sold jewellery and jugs, and a tiny post office which was also a supermarket. Fizza went up to the counter.

‘Do you sell newspapers?’ she asked a small grey-haired lady.

‘Sorry,’ she said, ‘they haven’t arrived from Guernsey today. Try tomorrow.’

‘What is this place?’ thought Fizza. ‘There aren’t even any newspapers!’

She thanked the lady and left the shop.

[3]______________________, she passed a group of girls of about her age. They were chewing gum and wearing short skirts. They looked just like the ‘cool’ girls from school, which made Fizza smile.

‘Some things never change,’ she thought, ‘wherever you go.’ And she began to run back towards the cottage.

[4]______________________, Fizza and her dad practised judo in the field behind the cottage. [5]______________________ they threw one another onto the grass until Imran admitted defeat and went inside to play a game of cards with Rubel.

As the sun began to drop down from the sky like a great big orange, Fizza continued to practise her judo moves. [6]______________________, she got tired and stopped. She looked out at the dark grey sea and breathed in deeply. And for the first time since she had arrived on Sark, she found herself listening. She could hear the birds singing goodnight to each other, and the sound of sheep bells and a boat in the distance. [7]______________________, she breathed in deeply and she found that the evening air of Sark smelled sweet. It was completely different from the heavy city smell of her much-loved Birmingham. Such beauty suddenly made Fizza McIntyre feel alive and she decided to show the island how good she felt.

‘Goodnight, Sark!’ she shouted as she jumped high in the air and then fell on the grass.

Laughing at herself for being silly, she picked herself up and turned to go indoors, but immediately she came to a stop.

Sitting in a tree beside the cottage was a red-haired boy who looked about the same age as her.

[8]______________________ they stared at one another until her attention was taken by a small brown rabbit that ran past her. She took her eyes away from the boy for just a few seconds and during this time he completely disappeared.

3 Read the rest of the extract again. Mark the statements T (true) or F (false).

1 The shop on the island never has newspapers. ☐
2 Fizza sees some girls who remind her of her school. ☐
3 Fizza and her father do judo together. ☐
4 Fizza thinks that the air on the island is like the air at home. ☐
5 She shouts 'Goodnight, Sark' because the island has made her feel good. ☐
6 The boy she sees is chasing a rabbit. ☐

4 SPEAKING Think about these questions. Then discuss your answers with other students.

Imagine you can travel somewhere that's completely different from where you live.

1 Where would you choose to go? Why?
2 What would you miss most about where you live now?

WRITING

A story about a bad decision

1 INPUT Read the story. What was Pauline's bad decision, according to the writer?

2 Find sentences in the story with these meanings. How are the underlined phrases expressed in the story?

1 Pauline regretted the fact that she'd gone to university.
2 It's a pity that you didn't tell us.
3 I think it's a pity that she didn't tell her parents.
4 It isn't good that Pauline didn't make her own decision.

3 ANALYSE The story has four paragraphs. Which of them:

a is about a decision that the person made?
b gives background information about the person?
c gives the writer's thoughts about the whole situation?
d explains the effects of the decision?

4 PRODUCE Think of a (true or invented) story about a bad decision. Write your story (200 words). Think about:

- who the person is / was.
- the situation the person was in which meant that he/she had to make a decision.
- the decision that the person made.
- what happened after making the decision.
- what you or the person felt about it all afterwards.

ABOUT BLOG LATEST POSTS ARCHIVES

LEARNING FROM EXPERIENCE?

We asked readers to tell us stories about bad decisions they or people they know have made.

Here's this week's story.

1 A friend of mine has a sister, Pauline, who's six years older than him. She was always good at school, but all she really wanted to do was to help her parents in their small shop, and then perhaps take it over when they were too old to run it.

2 Pauline's parents, however, really wanted her to go to university, so she spent three years at school working incredibly hard, studying for an exam for a famous university in another city. She passed, and a few months later she left home to start studying there.

3 From the first moment, Pauline wished she hadn't gone to university. She hated it. She'd been a clever student at school, but the university work was much harder. She didn't make many friends either, so she was lonely and homesick. After six months, she asked her parents to let her leave and come home. They were very surprised when she said that she'd never wanted to go to university. 'If only you'd told us!' they said. 'But I didn't want to disappoint you,' was her answer.

4 Now Pauline is working in the shop and she's very happy. I wish she'd told her parents that university wasn't what she wanted – then she wouldn't have wasted six months of her life. Pauline should have made her own decision.

READING AND USE OF ENGLISH

Gapped text

→ workbook page 115

1 You are going to read about someone travelling abroad for the first time. Six sentences have been removed from the text. Choose from the sentences (A–G) the one that fits each gap (1–6). There is one extra sentence that you do not need to use.

I've never really enjoyed travelling very much. The idea of leaving the comfort of my own bed to sleep somewhere else has never appealed to me. And when you add in things like the food and not being understood, the thought of leaving my hometown fills me with terror. I did go away on a school trip once, when I was eight, for two nights. My mother tells me I quite enjoyed the experience. 1 ______ There must be a reason why I can't remember anything positive about it.

So for 28 years I'd managed to lead a life that kept me happily at home. A few nights in hotels for work had been the worst I'd had to go through. Then, one day, my boss called me in. He shook my hand. He was smiling from one ear to the other. 2 ______ 'Paul!' he announced. 'You've been promoted.' I should have been happy, I suppose, but something in the back of my mind was telling me this wasn't 100 percent good news. 3 ______ 'Of course, you'll need extra training. I've booked you on a course at head office in Linz. Your flight's on Monday.'

I started to feel dizzy. I had to hold on to the table to stop myself from falling. My boss patted me on the back.

'Great news, eh?' he smiled. Then he left the room.

So that was it. Just when my professional life had got better, the rest of my life was over. No one had ever survived an aeroplane flight, had they? 4 ______ I wasn't so sure. I spent the weekend making my final farewells as Monday morning got closer.

5 ______ Before I knew it, my taxi had left me at the airport. Somehow I made my way to the check-in desk. I lifted my suitcase onto the conveyor belt and walked through airport security to the lounge. I have no idea how I knew what to do. I guess that because I'd seen it so many times in films, it was programmed into my mind.

The flight was only two hours. 6 ______ I tried to read a book, but I couldn't. I tried listening to my MP3 player – I'd chosen some relaxing music especially – but it sounded like it was being played by an orchestra of three-year-olds. Every sound the plane made sent my imagination spinning out of control. Was that the sound of the wing falling off? Was that a bird being sucked through an engine? Was that the noise of wheels hitting the runway? Yes, it was. We had landed.

Somehow we'd arrived. I wanted to grab my fellow travellers and celebrate the fact that we were still alive, but they were all busy getting their luggage from the overhead lockers. So I celebrated on my own.
But then I remembered: unless I wanted to spend the rest of my life in Austria, I still had to fly back!

A What wasn't right about this?
B My family and friends tried to assure me that of course they had.
C I thought that it was never going to end.
D And then the day I had been dreading arrived.
E Would I ever see my wife again?
F It wasn't long before I found out why.
G That certainly isn't what my memory tells me.

TEST YOURSELF UNITS 11 & 12

VOCABULARY

1 Complete the sentences with the words / phrases in the list. There are four extra words / phrases.

survived | afraid | illogical | work out | rescued | panicked | informal | dangerous
hang out | run into | coming around | irresponsible | impatient | made up

1 After she hit her head, she slowly started ____________ .
2 I can't come climbing with you. No way! I'm ____________ of heights.
3 The firefighter ____________ the cat from the tree.
4 The show didn't go very well – I ____________ when I walked on stage, and then I forgot what I wanted to say.
5 Luckily, everyone ____________ the plane crash last night.
6 Don't be so ____________ . It'll be your turn soon.
7 They ____________ that story. There is no way that it is true.
8 I can't ____________ the answer to this question. Can you help me?
9 It was very ____________ of you to go swimming in the sea during the storm.
10 When I'm in town, I often ____________ people I know.

/10

GRAMMAR

2 Complete the sentences with the words / phrases in the list. There are two extra words / phrases.

I wish | if | only | such | feel like | afford | so | in order to

1 It was ____________ a loud noise that everybody in the street heard it.
2 He jumped into the lake ____________ rescue the boy.
3 I don't ____________ going swimming. It's too cold.
4 He can't ____________ to buy that computer game. He owes Tom some money.
5 Everyone laughs at my hair. If ____________ I hadn't dyed it green!
6 ____________ you'd waited for me. Then this wouldn't have happened.

3 Find and correct the mistake in each sentence.

1 It's a complicated problem. We need to work out it.
2 I decided going out this evening.
3 I'm such hungry! I'll have to eat something now.
4 They're going to cover the hole so to prevent future accidents.
5 It was so a bad car crash that nobody survived.
6 After the accident, my dad promised wearing a seat belt in future.

/12

FUNCTIONAL LANGUAGE

4 Choose the correct words.

1 A The police want to increase the fine to £1,000 *for / to* stop people driving so fast.
B I think that's *so / such* a good idea.
2 A What's the *shame / matter*, Erika?
B I'm feeling a bit ill. I wish I *hadn't / haven't* eaten all that cake.
3 A Let's have a book sale *in / on* order to make some money for the school.
B That's not a bad *matter / idea*.
4 A His headache was *so / such* bad that he couldn't concentrate on the exam and failed.
B I'm sorry to hear *this / that*.

/8

MY SCORE /30

22–30 | 10–21 | 0–9

PRONUNCIATION

UNIT 1
Linking words with *up*

1 1.04 **Read and listen to the dialogue.**

Steve What's up, Jenny?
Jenny I'm tired! I'm up late every night studying.
Steve You need your sleep! Can't you get up later?
Jenny Not really. I've taken up the flute this year. I practise in the mornings.
Steve Well, it's up to you, but I'd give that up!
Jenny Hmmm … I wish I hadn't signed up for the school orchestra now!

2 **What happens to the words in blue? Choose the correct word to complete the rule:**

A word ending in a *consonant* / *vowel* sound links with the following word when it begins with a *consonant* / *vowel* sound.

3 1.05 **Listen, repeat and practise.**

UNIT 2
Initial consonant clusters with /s/

1 2.02 **Read and listen to the tongue twisters.**

Strong winds spread the sparks through the streets.
Stella's got straight hair and stripes on her skirt.
Stewart sprayed his phone with a special screen cleaner.

2 **Say the words with blue letters in them.**

3 2.03 **Listen, repeat and practise.**

UNIT 3
Strong and weak forms: /ɒv/ and /əv/

1 3.05 **Read and listen to the dialogue.**

Julia What do you always buy the same brand of?
Jack I always buy the same brand of trainers. They're called Ace. I bought a pair of green ones last week.
Julia Ace? What are they made of?
Jack They're made of fabric and rubber. They put a lot of effort into the design and quality of them.
Julia And into the marketing of them, too!

2 3.05 **Listen again and make a note of each of which is stressed and each of which is unstressed.**

3 3.06 **Listen, repeat and practise.**

UNIT 4
Consonant–vowel word linking

1 4.05 **Read and listen to the dialogue.**

Lisa I was only joking, but I wish I hadn't said it. I think she hates me.
Henry Well, it was unkind of you to say you didn't like her new haircut.
Lisa I know! I can't believe I said that she looked like a boy! It just came out. What should I do?
Henry First, I'd apologise. Then I'd admit that I prefer it long. Actually, I think she looks amazing!

2 4.05 **Find examples of linking in the dialogue. Then listen and check.**

3 4.06 **Listen, repeat and practise.**

UNIT 5
The schwa /ə/ in word endings

1 5.06 **Read and listen to the tongue twisters.**

Ireland's a nation with famous traditions.
My neighbour's a brilliant classical musician.
The monster's a villain who frightens the children.

2 5.06 **Listen again and focus on the syllables in blue. Are they stressed or unstressed? They all have the same short vowel sound. What is it?**

3 5.07 **Listen, repeat and practise.**

UNIT 6
The /ʒ/ phoneme

1 6.02 **Read and listen to the interview.**

Helen Welcome to *Film Night Television*. Our guest is Tom Potts, who stars in an unusual thriller called *Asian Treasure*. Why did you decide to take on this role?
Tom It was a difficult decision, Helen. I play the part of an amazing illusionist.
Helen There are so many collisions and explosions in the film that I thought you would never find that treasure.
Tom It's true! Occasionally I was frightened for my own life!

2 6.02 **How is each 's' in blue pronounced?**

3 6.03 **Listen, repeat and practise.**

UNIT 7

Intonation – inviting, accepting and refusing invitations

1 7.05 **Read and listen to the dialogue.**

Max Hi, Gina! I'm organising a hiking trip. Why don't you come along?

Gina Thank you, Max. I'd love to. When are you going?

Max Next Saturday. We're going to climb Mount Sunrise. How about bringing some friends?

Gina That's a great idea! Oh … I'm already going out on Saturday. What a shame. I'm sorry, Max.

2 7.05 **Make a note of the two invitations and the sentences where Gina accepts and refuses the invitation. What happens to Max and Gina's voice in each case? Listen again and check.**

3 7.06 **Listen, repeat and practise.**

UNIT 8

Intonation – expressing surprise

1 8.06 **Read and listen to the dialogue.**

Jackson You're not going to believe this.

Maryanne Tell me.

Jackson School's closed for the rest of the term!

Maryanne What?

Jackson The police said there was an urgent situation but didn't give any details.

Maryanne That's awful!

Jackson And the head teacher said she's extremely sorry but there's nothing she can do!

Maryanne Really?

2 8.06 **Listen again and write down all of the words which are stressed.**

3 8.07 **Listen, repeat and practise.**

UNIT 9

Moving word stress

1 9.02 **Read and listen to the dialogues.**

1 A Do you know the **mystery** of Amelia Earhart?
B Yes – her disappearance is very **mysterious**!

2 A Wow! That's a great **photograph**.
B Thanks! I'm really into **photography**.

3 A If we go to this summer camp, we can do the course on **navigation**.
B But I already know how to **navigate**.

2 **Find the stressed syllables in the words in blue. Say the two words in blue in each dialogue.**

3 9.03 **Listen, repeat and practise.**

UNIT 10

Short and long vowel sounds: /ɪ/ – /iː/ and /ɒ/ – /əʊ/

1 10.03 **Read and listen to the dialogues.**

Mrs Green We all need good self esteem. But what does it mean? Tim?

Tim It's a lot of things, Mrs Green. But it's really important to feel happy to be as we are.

Mr Ross So, do you copy your favourite pop stars? Do you wear the same clothes, Rose?

Rose Mr Ross! I follow pop stars – but I don't wear the same clothes! I'm not a clone.

2 **Say the words with the *short* /ɪ/ and the *long* /iː/ sounds. How does your mouth change shape? Say the words with the *short* /ɒ/ and the *long* /əʊ/ sounds. How does your mouth change shape now?**

3 10.04 **Listen, repeat and practise.**

UNIT 11

Strong and weak forms: /tuː/ and /tə/

1 11.02 **Read and listen to the dialogue.**

Steve Hi, Jane! It's good **to** see you. What have you been up **to**?

Jane I've been travelling. I've been **to** so many places, I couldn't name them all!

Steve Wow, that's exciting. Did you go **to** Germany?

Jane Well … that's one place I didn't get **to**. I went **to** France and Spain, though.

2 **Say the words in blue with the weak form of *to*. Now say the words in red in the strong form.**

3 11.03 **Listen, repeat and practise.**

UNIT 12

Different pronunciations of *ea*

1 12.04 **Read and listen to the dialogue.**

Teacher Has everyone **read** the article about **healthy** living?

Jean I have, sir. From the **research** I **learned** that we have to look after ourselves from an **early** age.

Teacher Yes, it would **appear** that every **year** counts. Are there any more **ideas**?

Heather **Eating** and sleeping well is **really** important, Mr **Heath**.

Teacher **Great** answer. Now let's take a **break**!

2 **How many different pronunciations of the *ea* spelling are there? Say the highlighted words.**

3 12.05 **Listen, repeat and practise.**

GET IT RIGHT!

UNIT 1

Present simple vs. present continuous

It's common to confuse the present simple and present continuous.

We use the present simple to describe facts, routine activities and opinions.

✓ *I **usually go** there on foot.*

✗ *I ~~'m usually going~~ there on foot.*

We use the present continuous to describe events that are happening now or around now.

✓ *I**'m sending** you a photo of my new bike.*

✗ *I ~~send~~ you a photo of my new bike.*

Find the error in each of these sentences. Rewrite the sentences correctly.

0 I know how hard you try to get on the team.
I know how hard you are trying to get on the team.

1 I think I am the person you look for.

____

2 I'm playing tennis on Tuesdays.

____

3 At the moment I write a letter to a friend.

____

4 I like what you wear today.

____

5 I know what you mean and are appreciating your help.

____

6 We are playing football during most school breaks.

____

UNIT 2

Present perfect vs. past simple

Students often confuse the present perfect and past simple tenses.

We use the past simple when we include a past time expression to say when in the past an event took place.

✓ *Yesterday I **ate** rice.*

✗ *Yesterday I ~~have eaten~~ rice.*

We use the present perfect to talk about past events when we don't say exactly when they took place and with expressions such as *yet, before, ever* and *never*.

✓ *I**'ve** never **been** to London before.*

✗ *I ~~didn't go~~ to London before.*

Make sentences using the prompts below.

0 we / see / the advertisement at the bus stop / yesterday
We saw the advertisement at the bus stop yesterday.

1 I / not see / the new Hobbit film / yet

____

2 you / ever / go / to Spain?

____

3 John / take / his exam / last week

____

4 Nina / get / here / a few minutes ago

____

5 they / not eat / at this restaurant / before

____

6 I / not eat / breakfast / so I'm really hungry and it's two hours till lunchtime!

____

Past continuous vs. past simple

Learners sometimes confuse the past continuous with the past simple.
✓ *I was happy when I **came** first in the race.*
✗ *I was happy when I ~~was coming~~ first in the race.*

Which of these sentences are correct and which are incorrect? Rewrite the incorrect ones.

0 Last time I was visiting the library, I couldn't find the book I was looking for.
Last time I visited the library, I couldn't find the book I was looking for.

1 When she arrived, I cooked dinner so I was a bit distracted.
______

2 After that, I watched TV for about an hour.
______

3 As usual, we were arriving at about 6 pm; then we had dinner.
______

4 My teacher came to see how our project went.
______

5 I'll never forget the time I was spending in Nepal.
______

6 The police saw the men and asked them what they did there.
______

UNIT 3

have to vs. *had to*

Learners sometimes confuse *have to* and *had to*.
We use *have to* to talk about an obligation in the present, and *had to* to talk about an obligation in the past.
✓ *Shopping is stressful, especially if you **have to** find a particular item of clothing.*
✗ *Shopping is stressful, especially if you ~~had to~~ find a particular item of clothing.*

Which of these sentences are correct and which are incorrect? Rewrite the incorrect ones.

0 The trains were fully booked so we have to forget about that trip.
The trains were fully booked so we had to forget about that trip.

1 I'm sorry I can't attend class tomorrow because I had to go to the doctor.
______

2 My dad was going to work for another company so we have to move house.
______

3 If you want a drink after swimming, you have to go somewhere else.
______

4 If I have to choose between going to a small school or a large one, I would choose a large one.
______

5 Do we have to bring any money for the trip next week?
______

6 Yesterday we had to write an essay about Barack Obama.
______

don't have to vs. *mustn't*

Learners sometimes make errors with *don't have to* and *mustn't*.
Although *have to* and *must* both mean something is necessary, *don't have to* means that something is not necessary, whereas *mustn't* means that something is prohibited.
✓ *I **don't have to** work tonight, as I've already finished everything.*
✗ *I ~~mustn't~~ work tonight, as I've already finished everything.*
✓ *I **mustn't** fail my exam, or I'll have to retake it.*

Write the sentences with *mustn't* or *don't have to*.

0 You / stay out late or you'll be really tired tomorrow.
You mustn't stay out late or you'll be really tired tomorrow.

1 You / finish your essay now. Mr Jenkins said that we can hand it in next Friday.
______

2 You / bring anything to the party – just bring yourself!
______

3 You / eat food in class – it's against the rules.
______

4 You / talk during exams.
______

5 You / revise every unit. The exam only includes Units 1 to 3.
______

6 You / use your phone in class. It'll be confiscated.
______

UNIT 4

if vs. *when*

Learners often confuse *if* with *when*.

We use *if* to indicate possible actions or events.

✓ *It'll be best for us **if** everyone goes by bicycle. Car parking facilities are limited.*

✗ *It'll be best for us ~~when~~ everyone goes by bicycle. Car parking facilities are limited.*

We use *when* to indicate events which have happened in the past or are going to happen in the future.

✓ *I can pass on your message. I'll tell him **when** I see him tomorrow.*

✗ *I can pass on your message. I'll tell him ~~if~~ I see him tomorrow.*

Complete these sentences with *if* or *when*.

0 I was very pleased ___*when*___ I read your letter.
1 I had a great time ____________ I went to New York.
2 Would it be OK ____________ I invited my friend?
3 I'll call you ____________ I get home tonight.
4 Do you mind ____________ we meet at 5 pm instead of 4 pm?
5 ____________ you're free on Saturday, come to the cinema with us!
6 He went to Africa ____________ he was 21 because of his job.
7 How much would it cost ____________ we were a group of ten?

UNIT 5

Relative pronouns

Learners sometimes confuse *who* and *which*.

We use *who* to refer to people and *which* to refer to things.

✓ *Next week I'm going to visit my Uncle Joe, **who** lives in Manchester.*

✗ *Next week I'm going to visit my Uncle Joe, ~~which~~ lives in Manchester.*

Complete the sentences with *who* or *which*.

0 There are several problems ___*which*___ can't wait any longer.
1 My friend Paul, ____________ I've known since primary school, is coming.
2 Animals ____________ can protect themselves shouldn't be kept in a zoo.
3 My dad works for a company ____________ sells dental products.
4 It's a great film but it's really sad. It's about a soldier ____________ goes to war.
5 She was the only one ____________ talked to me.
6 He's currently working for a charity ____________ helps elderly people.

UNIT 6

absolutely vs. *very*

A common mistake is using intensifiers like *absolutely* and *very* with the wrong types of adjectives.

We use *absolutely* to modify non-gradable adjectives or adjectives with a strong or extreme meaning.

✓ *It's **absolutely** delicious.*

✗ *It's ~~very~~ delicious.*

We use *very* to modify gradable adjectives.

✓ *I was **very** disappointed with it.*

✗ *I was ~~absolutely~~ disappointed with it.*

Complete the sentences with *absolutely* or *very*.

0 In my opinion, the countryside is ___*very*___ relaxing.
1 This museum is ____________ fascinating.
2 The view from the top was ____________ amazing.
3 I thought the documentary was ____________ interesting.
4 I was ____________ thrilled to get an 'A' on that assignment.
5 This food is ____________ tasty.
6 She's a ____________ good singer.

UNIT 7

make vs. *let*

Learners sometimes confuse *make* and *let* in phrases such as *let me know*.

✓ *You were on TV and you didn't **let** us know!*

✗ *You were on TV and you didn't ~~make~~ us know!*

Complete the sentences with the correct form of *make* or *let*.

0 There are great views which will ___*make*___ you feel very comfortable.
1 ____________ me help you with that bag. It looks really heavy.
2 The band came on stage late. They ____________ us wait over an hour.
3 That TV documentary about diet and health really ____________ me think about doing more exercise.
4 Mum, can you write a note to my teacher to ____________ her know why I won't be in class tomorrow?
5 It's so important to ____________ people aware of the disease so that we can raise money to help prevent it.
6 It was very kind of you to ____________ us stay over, Mrs Johnson. Thanks very much for having us!

UNIT 8
say vs. *tell*

Learners sometimes confuse *say* and *tell*.
The meaning of *say* and *tell* is exactly the same but we use them differently.
We *tell someone* (*something*) and we *say something* (*to someone*).
✓ *I didn't **say anything to** my brother about it.*
✗ *I didn't ~~tell anything to~~ my brother about it.*

We can also use a *that* clause immediately after *tell*, but not after *say*.
✓ ***Tell her that** I'll phone her.*
✗ *~~Say her that~~ I'll phone her.*

There are some collocations we can use with *tell* that don't follow the above rules: we can *tell a lie* / *the truth* / *a story*.

Complete each of these sentences with the correct form of *say* or *tell*.

0 Everybody ___*said*___ something about himself, and so did I.
1 I have to ____________ that this is a great piece of writing. Well done!
2 You're going to have to ____________ him that you can't play in Saturday's match. You're injured.
3 ____________ us the story of how you met.
4 Did he ____________ why he lied?
5 My mum ____________ that we were going to move house.
6 I'd like to ____________ a big thank you for all your help this year.
7 I knew that he ____________ the truth.

UNIT 9
Modals of deduction in the present

It is a common error to use *can* as a present modal of deduction, where *could* is required. In the negative, however, it is possible to use *can't* as well as *couldn't*.
✓ *I'm not sure why they decided not to buy tickets to see the band, but it **could be** due to lack of money.*
✗ *I'm not sure why they decided not to buy tickets to see the band, but it ~~can be~~ due to lack of money.*
✓ *The reason **can't be** a lack of interest.*

Which of these sentences are correct and which are incorrect? Rewrite the incorrect ones.

0 Where's John? He can be at home.
Where's John? He could be at home.

1 A Do you have a better idea for how to get there?
B Well, I think another route can be better.
____

2 A Does he need help?
B He can do. It looks like he might be waving for us to stop.
____

3 A How does that car go so fast?
B It can be because it's so light. Just a guess!
____

4 A What do you think is going to happen in the game?
B They could still win or maybe it'll be a draw.
____

5 A Is Dad still at work?
B The car's outside. He can't be.
____

6 A Who made the complaint?
B It could be Nick – he didn't think there was a problem.
____

UNIT 10
Future continuous vs. future simple

Learners often confuse the future continuous with the future simple.
We use the future continuous to talk about events which will be in the process of happening at some time in the future.
✓ *This time next week **I'll be sitting** on the beach in Cádiz.*
✗ *This time next week ~~I'll sit~~ on the beach in Cádiz.*

Decide if the sentences *can* be written in the future continuous. If so, rewrite them using this tense. What's the difference in meaning between the future simple and future continuous form in these cases?

0 When you get to the station, I'll wait for you at the main entrance.
When you get to the station, I'll be waiting for you at the main entrance.

1 This time next year we'll be at university and we'll live away from home.
____

2 I'll have a look in my diary and see if I'm free on the 5th.
____

3 This time next week I'll do my final exams. Scary!
____

4 Some people think that tablets will soon replace laptops.
____

5 I'll play hockey when you arrive at the station tomorrow but Chloë can meet you.

____

6 I think you'll have a good time when you go to Spain.

____

UNIT 11
Verb patterns

Learners sometimes make errors with verb patterns, using *to* + infinitive when it should be a gerund and vice versa.

✓ I ***don't mind going*** *home first.*

✗ I ~~don't mind to go~~ *home first.*

Which of these sentences are correct and which are incorrect? Rewrite the incorrect ones.

0 He's always had problems to focus on one task.
He's always had problems focusing on one task.

1 Do you need more time finishing your work?

____

2 Lately I've been spending a lot of time to watch TV.

____

3 I need to start working on my essay as soon as possible.

____

4 It was a very heavy film, but we enjoyed to learn about history.

____

5 It's best studying new vocabulary regularly.

____

6 I had real difficulties downloading this app but I got there eventually.

____

UNIT 12
Phrasal verbs

Learners sometimes avoid using phrasal verbs, using single, often Latinate, verbs instead. Using phrasal verbs can make you sound more natural and increase the variety of your English.

✓✓ *Students were* ***put up*** *in hotels.*

✓ *Students were* ***accommodated*** *in hotels.*

Replace the verbs in bold with phrasal verbs from the list.

put up with | put on | put up (x3) | put off

0 Before I went to the beach, I **applied** sun cream.
Before I went to the beach, I put on sun cream.

1 Our family has agreed to **host** a foreign student for a month during the summer.

____

2 One advantage of taking the train is that you don't have to **tolerate** traffic jams.

____

3 I don't get to exercise so much any more and I'm worried about **gaining** weight.

____

4 Good news! We're going to have to **postpone** today's test until next Friday.

____

5 Cinema tickets were already expensive and now they've just **increased** the prices again.

____

6 We **displayed** posters to advertise the event.

____

STUDENT A

UNIT 1, PAGE 18

Student A
You aren't very happy with your brother or sister. He/She plays loud music that you don't like when you're trying to work. He/She doesn't even keep the door closed. What else upsets you about this? You have decided to talk to him/her about it. Try and use the expressions in Exercise 5.
Excuse me, [name], I need a word ...

UNIT 7, PAGE 72

Student A

1 Invite your partner to do these things with you. Then add one more idea of your own.
- Watch a football match at the local sports ground.
- Meet some of your friends and go to the shopping centre.

2 Accept or refuse your partner's invitations.

STUDENT B

UNIT 1, PAGE 18

Student B

You aren't very happy with your brother or sister. He/She keeps taking your clothes without asking you. He/She makes a real mess when he/she takes them from your wardrobe. What else upsets you about this? You have decided to talk to him/her about it. Try and use the expressions in Exercise 5.

Excuse me, [name], I need a word ...

UNIT 7, PAGE 72

Student B

1 Accept or refuse your partner's invitations.

2 Invite your partner to do these things with you. Then add one more idea of your own.

- Watch a horror DVD at your place.
- Go for a long walk in the mountains.